JULIUS CAESAR

WILLIAM SHAKESPEARE

Published by True Sign Publishing House
Address: SY. No. 21/2 & 21/3, Sonnenahalli,
Krishnarajapura, Bengaluru,
Karnataka - 560049 India
E-mail: truesignbooks@gmail.com
Website: www.truesign.in

Julius Caesar

Author: William Shakespeare

ISBN: 978-93-5462-967-9

First Edition: 2022

Contents

Dramatis Personæ

JULIUS CAESAR	
OCTAVIUS CAESAR	Triumvir after his death.
MARCUS ANTONIUS, " " "	M. AEMILIUS LEPIDUS, " " "
CICERO, PUBLIUS,	
POPILIUS LENA	Senators.
MARCUS BRUTUS	Conspirator against Caesar.
CASSIUS, " " "	
CASCA, " " "	
TREBONIUS, " " "	
LIGARIUS," " "	
DECIUS BRUTUS, " " "	
METELLUS CIMBER, " " "	
CINNA, " " "	
FLAVIUS	tribune
MARULLUS	tribune
ARTEMIDORUS	a Sophist of Cnidos. A Soothsayer
CINNA	a poet. Another Poet.
LUCILIUS, TITINIUS,	
MESSALA,	young CATO,
and VOLUMNIUS	Friends to Brutus and Cassius.
VARRO, CLITUS,	
CLAUDIUS, STRATO,	
LUCIUS, DARDANIUS,	Servants to Brutus
PINDARUS	Servant to Cassius
CALPHURNIA,	wife to Caesar
PORTIA	wife to Brutus
	The Ghost of Caesar

Senators, Citizens, Soldiers, Commoners, Messengers, and Servants.

SCENE: Rome, the conspirators' camp near Sardis, and the plains of Philippi.

ACT-I
SCENE-I — Rome. A street

Enter FLAVIUS, MARULLUS *and a throng of* CITIZENS.

FLAVIUS
Hence! home, you idle creatures, get you home.
Is this a holiday? What, know you not,
Being mechanical, you ought not walk
Upon a labouring day without the sign
Of your profession? Speak, what trade art thou?

CARPENTER
Why, sir, a carpenter.

MARULLUS
Where is thy leather apron and thy rule?
What dost thou with thy best apparel on?
You, sir, what trade are you?

COBBLER
Truly, sir, in respect of a fine workman, I am but, as you would say, a cobbler.

MARULLUS
But what trade art thou? Answer me directly.

COBBLER
A trade, sir, that I hope I may use with a safe conscience, which is indeed, sir, a mender of bad soles.

MARULLUS
What trade, thou knave? Thou naughty knave, what trade?

COBBLER
Nay, I beseech you, sir, be not out with me; yet, if you be out, sir, I can mend you.

MARULLUS
What mean'st thou by that? Mend me, thou saucy fellow!

COBBLER
Why, sir, cobble you.

FLAVIUS
Thou art a cobbler, art thou?

COBBLER
Truly, sir, all that I live by is with the awl; I meddle with no tradesman's matters, nor women's matters, but withal I am indeed, sir, a surgeon to old shoes:

when they are in great danger, I recover them. As proper men as ever trod upon neat's leather have gone upon my handiwork.

FLAVIUS But wherefore art not in thy shop today?
Why dost thou lead these men about the streets?

COBBLER Truly, sir, to wear out their shoes, to get myself into more work. But indeed, sir, we make holiday to see Caesar, and to rejoice in his triumph.

MARULLUS Wherefore rejoice? What conquest brings he home?
What tributaries follow him to Rome,
To grace in captive bonds his chariot wheels?
You blocks, you stones, you worse than senseless things!
O you hard hearts, you cruel men of Rome,
Knew you not Pompey? Many a time and oft
Have you climb'd up to walls and battlements,
To towers and windows, yea, to chimney tops,
Your infants in your arms, and there have sat
The livelong day with patient expectation,
To see great Pompey pass the streets of Rome.
And when you saw his chariot but appear,
Have you not made an universal shout,
That Tiber trembled underneath her banks
To hear the replication of your sounds
Made in her concave shores?
And do you now put on your best attire?
And do you now cull out a holiday?
And do you now strew flowers in his way,
That comes in triumph over Pompey's blood?
Be gone!
Run to your houses, fall upon your knees,
Pray to the gods to intermit the plague
That needs must light on this ingratitude.

FLAVIUS Go, go, good countrymen, and, for this fault
Assemble all the poor men of your sort,
Draw them to Tiber banks, and weep your tears
Into the channel, till the lowest stream
Do kiss the most exalted shores of all.

[*Exeunt* CITIZENS.]

See whether their basest metal be not mov'd;
They vanish tongue-tied in their guiltiness.
Go you down that way towards the Capitol;
This way will I. Disrobe the images,
If you do find them deck'd with ceremonies.

MARULLUS May we do so?
You know it is the feast of Lupercal.

FLAVIUS It is no matter; let no images
Be hung with Caesar's trophies. I'll about
And drive away the vulgar from the streets;
So do you too, where you perceive them thick.
These growing feathers pluck'd from Caesar's wing
Will make him fly an ordinary pitch,
Who else would soar above the view of men,
And keep us all in servile fearfulness.

[*Exeunt.*]

SCENE-II — The same. A public place

Enter, in procession, with music, CAESAR; ANTONY, *for the course;* CALPHURNIA, PORTIA, DECIUS, CICERO, BRUTUS, CASSIUS *and* CASCA; *a great crowd following, among them a Soothsayer.*

CAESAR Calphurnia.

CASCA Peace, ho! Caesar speaks.

[*Music ceases.*]

CAESAR Calphurnia.

CALPHURNIA Here, my lord.

CAESAR Stand you directly in Antonius' way,
When he doth run his course. Antonius.

ANTONY Caesar, my lord?

CAESAR Forget not in your speed, Antonius,
To touch Calphurnia; for our elders say,
The barren, touched in this holy chase,
Shake off their sterile curse.

ANTONY I shall remember.
When Caesar says "Do this," it is perform'd.

CAESAR Set on; and leave no ceremony out.

[*Music.*]

SOOTHSAYER Caesar!

CAESAR Ha! Who calls?

CASCA Bid every noise be still; peace yet again!

[*Music ceases.*]

CAESAR Who is it in the press that calls on me?
I hear a tongue shriller than all the music,
Cry "Caesar"! Speak. Caesar is turn'd to hear.

SOOTHSAYER	Beware the Ides of March.
CAESAR	What man is that?
BRUTUS	A soothsayer bids you beware the Ides of March.
CAESAR	Set him before me; let me see his face.
CASSIUS	Fellow, come from the throng; look upon Caesar.
CAESAR	What say'st thou to me now? Speak once again.
SOOTHSAYER	Beware the Ides of March.
CAESAR	He is a dreamer; let us leave him. Pass.

[*Sennet. Exeunt all but* BRUTUS *and* CASSIUS.]

CASSIUS	Will you go see the order of the course?
BRUTUS	Not I.
CASSIUS	I pray you, do.
BRUTUS	I am not gamesome: I do lack some part Of that quick spirit that is in Antony. Let me not hinder, Cassius, your desires; I'll leave you.
CASSIUS	Brutus, I do observe you now of late: I have not from your eyes that gentleness And show of love as I was wont to have. You bear too stubborn and too strange a hand Over your friend that loves you.
BRUTUS	Cassius, Be not deceived: if I have veil'd my look, I turn the trouble of my countenance Merely upon myself. Vexed I am Of late with passions of some difference, Conceptions only proper to myself, Which give some soil perhaps to my behaviors; But let not therefore my good friends be grieved (Among which number, Cassius, be you one) Nor construe any further my neglect, Than that poor Brutus, with himself at war, Forgets the shows of love to other men.
CASSIUS	Then, Brutus, I have much mistook your passion; By means whereof this breast of mine hath buried Thoughts of great value, worthy cogitations. Tell me, good Brutus, can you see your face?

BRUTUS No, Cassius, for the eye sees not itself
But by reflection, by some other thing.

CASSIUS 'Tis just:
And it is very much lamented, Brutus,
That you have no such mirrors as will turn
Your hidden worthiness into your eye,
That you might see your shadow. I have heard
Where many of the best respect in Rome,
(Except immortal Caesar) speaking of Brutus,
And groaning underneath this age's yoke,
Have wish'd that noble Brutus had his eyes.

BRUTUS Into what dangers would you lead me, Cassius,
That you would have me seek into myself
For that which is not in me?

CASSIUS Therefore, good Brutus, be prepared to hear;
And since you know you cannot see yourself
So well as by reflection, I, your glass,
Will modestly discover to yourself
That of yourself which you yet know not of.
And be not jealous on me, gentle Brutus:
Were I a common laugher, or did use
To stale with ordinary oaths my love
To every new protester; if you know
That I do fawn on men, and hug them hard,
And after scandal them; or if you know
That I profess myself in banqueting,
To all the rout, then hold me dangerous.

[*Flourish and shout.*]

BRUTUS What means this shouting? I do fear the people
Choose Caesar for their king.

CASSIUS Ay, do you fear it?
Then must I think you would not have it so.

BRUTUS I would not, Cassius; yet I love him well,
But wherefore do you hold me here so long?
What is it that you would impart to me?
If it be aught toward the general good,
Set honour in one eye and death i' the other,
And I will look on both indifferently;

For let the gods so speed me as I love
The name of honour more than I fear death.

CASSIUS

I know that virtue to be in you, Brutus,
As well as I do know your outward favour.
Well, honour is the subject of my story.
I cannot tell what you and other men
Think of this life; but, for my single self,
I had as lief not be as live to be
In awe of such a thing as I myself.
I was born free as Caesar; so were you;
We both have fed as well, and we can both
Endure the winter's cold as well as he:
For once, upon a raw and gusty day,
The troubled Tiber chafing with her shores,
Caesar said to me, "Dar'st thou, Cassius, now
Leap in with me into this angry flood,
And swim to yonder point?" Upon the word,
Accoutred as I was, I plunged in,
And bade him follow: so indeed he did.
The torrent roar'd, and we did buffet it
With lusty sinews, throwing it aside
And stemming it with hearts of controversy.
But ere we could arrive the point propos'd,
Caesar cried, "Help me, Cassius, or I sink!"
I, as Aeneas, our great ancestor,
Did from the flames of Troy upon his shoulder
The old Anchises bear, so from the waves of Tiber
Did I the tired Caesar. And this man
Is now become a god; and Cassius is
A wretched creature, and must bend his body,
If Caesar carelessly but nod on him.
He had a fever when he was in Spain,
And when the fit was on him I did mark
How he did shake: 'tis true, this god did shake:
His coward lips did from their colour fly,
And that same eye whose bend doth awe the world
Did lose his lustre. I did hear him groan:
Ay, and that tongue of his, that bade the Romans
Mark him, and write his speeches in their books,
Alas, it cried, "Give me some drink, Titinius,"

As a sick girl. Ye gods, it doth amaze me,
A man of such a feeble temper should
So get the start of the majestic world,
And bear the palm alone.

[*Shout. Flourish.*]

BRUTUS
Another general shout?
I do believe that these applauses are
For some new honours that are heap'd on Caesar.

CASSIUS
Why, man, he doth bestride the narrow world
Like a Colossus, and we petty men
Walk under his huge legs, and peep about
To find ourselves dishonourable graves.
Men at some time are masters of their fates:
The fault, dear Brutus, is not in our stars,
But in ourselves, that we are underlings.
"Brutus" and "Caesar": what should be in that "Caesar"?
Why should that name be sounded more than yours?
Write them together, yours is as fair a name;
Sound them, it doth become the mouth as well;
Weigh them, it is as heavy; conjure with 'em,
"Brutus" will start a spirit as soon as "Caesar."
Now in the names of all the gods at once,
Upon what meat doth this our Caesar feed,
That he is grown so great? Age, thou art sham'd!
Rome, thou hast lost the breed of noble bloods!
When went there by an age since the great flood,
But it was fam'd with more than with one man?
When could they say, till now, that talk'd of Rome,
That her wide walls encompass'd but one man?
Now is it Rome indeed, and room enough,
When there is in it but one only man.
O, you and I have heard our fathers say,
There was a Brutus once that would have brook'd
Th' eternal devil to keep his state in Rome,
As easily as a king!

BRUTUS
That you do love me, I am nothing jealous;
What you would work me to, I have some aim:

How I have thought of this, and of these times,
I shall recount hereafter. For this present,
I would not, so with love I might entreat you,
Be any further mov'd. What you have said,
I will consider; what you have to say
I will with patience hear; and find a time
Both meet to hear and answer such high things.
Till then, my noble friend, chew upon this:
Brutus had rather be a villager
Than to repute himself a son of Rome
Under these hard conditions as this time
Is like to lay upon us.

CASSIUS I am glad that my weak words
Have struck but thus much show of fire from
Brutus.

Enter CAESAR *and his Train.*

BRUTUS The games are done, and Caesar is returning.

CASSIUS As they pass by, pluck Casca by the sleeve,
And he will, after his sour fashion, tell you
What hath proceeded worthy note today.

BRUTUS I will do so. But, look you, Cassius,
The angry spot doth glow on Caesar's brow,
And all the rest look like a chidden train:
Calphurnia's cheek is pale; and Cicero
Looks with such ferret and such fiery eyes
As we have seen him in the Capitol,
Being cross'd in conference by some senators.

CASSIUS Casca will tell us what the matter is.

CAESAR Antonius.

ANTONY Caesar?

CAESAR Let me have men about me that are fat,
Sleek-headed men, and such as sleep a-nights:
Yond Cassius has a lean and hungry look;
He thinks too much: such men are dangerous.

ANTONY Fear him not, Caesar; he's not dangerous;
He is a noble Roman and well given.

CAESAR Would he were fatter! But I fear him not:

Yet if my name were liable to fear,
I do not know the man I should avoid
So soon as that spare Cassius. He reads much,
He is a great observer, and he looks
Quite through the deeds of men. He loves no plays,
As thou dost, Antony; he hears no music.
Seldom he smiles; and smiles in such a sort
As if he mock'd himself and scorn'd his spirit
That could be mov'd to smile at anything.
Such men as he be never at heart's ease
Whiles they behold a greater than themselves,
And therefore are they very dangerous.
I rather tell thee what is to be fear'd
Than what I fear; for always I am Caesar.
Come on my right hand, for this ear is deaf,
And tell me truly what thou think'st of him.

[*Exeunt* CAESAR *and his Train.* CASCA *stays.*]

CASCA You pull'd me by the cloak; would you speak with me?

BRUTUS Ay, Casca, tell us what hath chanc'd today,
That Caesar looks so sad.

CASCA Why, you were with him, were you not?

BRUTUS I should not then ask Casca what had chanc'd.

CASCA Why, there was a crown offer'd him; and being offer'd him, he put it by with the back of his hand, thus; and then the people fell a-shouting.

BRUTUS What was the second noise for?

CASCA Why, for that too.

CASSIUS They shouted thrice: what was the last cry for?

CASCA Why, for that too.

BRUTUS Was the crown offer'd him thrice?

CASCA Ay, marry, was't, and he put it by thrice, every time gentler than other; and at every putting-by mine honest neighbours shouted.

CASSIUS Who offer'd him the crown?

CASCA Why, Antony.

BRUTUS Tell us the manner of it, gentle Casca.

CASCA I can as well be hang'd, as tell the manner of it: it was mere foolery; I did not mark it. I saw Mark Antony offer him a crown; yet 'twas not a crown neither, 'twas one of these coronets; and, as I told you, he put it by once: but, for all that, to my thinking, he would fain have had it. Then he offered it to him again: then he put it by again: but, to my thinking, he was very loath to lay his fingers off it. And then he offered it the third time; he put it the third time by; and still, as he refus'd it, the rabblement hooted, and clapp'd their chopt hands, and threw up their sweaty night-caps, and uttered such a deal of stinking breath because Caesar refus'd the crown, that it had, almost, choked Caesar, for he swooned, and fell down at it. And for mine own part, I durst not laugh, for fear of opening my lips and receiving the bad air.

CASSIUS But, soft! I pray you. What, did Caesar swoon?

CASCA He fell down in the market-place, and foam'd at mouth, and was speechless.

BRUTUS 'Tis very like: he hath the falling-sickness.

CASSIUS No, Caesar hath it not; but you, and I,
And honest Casca, we have the falling-sickness.

CASCA I know not what you mean by that; but I am sure Caesar fell down. If the tag-rag people did not clap him and hiss him, according as he pleased and displeased them, as they use to do the players in the theatre, I am no true man.

BRUTUS What said he when he came unto himself?

CASCA Marry, before he fell down, when he perceived the common herd was glad he refused the crown, he pluck'd me ope his doublet, and offer'd them his throat to cut. And I had been a man of any occupation, if I would not have taken him at a word, I would I might go to hell among the rogues. And so he fell. When he came to himself again, he said, if he had done or said anything amiss, he desir'd their worships to think it was his infirmity. Three or four wenches where I stood cried, "Alas, good soul!" and forgave him with all their hearts. But there's no heed to be taken of them: if Caesar had stabb'd their mothers, they would have done no less.

BRUTUS And, after that, he came thus sad away?

CASCA Ay.

CASSIUS Did Cicero say anything?

CASCA Ay, he spoke Greek.

CASSIUS To what effect?

CASCA Nay, and I tell you that, I'll ne'er look you i' the face again. But those that understood him smil'd at one another and shook their heads; but for mine own part, it was Greek to me. I could tell you more news too: Marullus and Flavius, for pulling scarfs off Caesar's images, are put to silence. Fare you well. There was more foolery yet, if I could remember it.

CASSIUS Will you sup with me tonight, Casca?

CASCA No, I am promis'd forth.

CASSIUS Will you dine with me tomorrow?

CASCA Ay, if I be alive, and your mind hold, and your dinner worth the eating.

CASSIUS Good. I will expect you.

CASCA Do so; farewell both.

[*Exit* CASCA.]

BRUTUS What a blunt fellow is this grown to be!
He was quick mettle when he went to school.

CASSIUS So is he now in execution
Of any bold or noble enterprise,
However he puts on this tardy form.
This rudeness is a sauce to his good wit,
Which gives men stomach to digest his words
With better appetite.

BRUTUS And so it is. For this time I will leave you:
Tomorrow, if you please to speak with me,
I will come home to you; or, if you will,
Come home to me, and I will wait for you.

CASSIUS I will do so: till then, think of the world.

[*Exit* BRUTUS.]

Well, Brutus, thou art noble; yet I see,
Thy honourable metal may be wrought
From that it is dispos'd: therefore 'tis meet
That noble minds keep ever with their likes;
For who so firm that cannot be seduc'd?
Caesar doth bear me hard, but he loves Brutus.
If I were Brutus now, and he were Cassius,
He should not humour me. I will this night,
In several hands, in at his windows throw,
As if they came from several citizens,
Writings, all tending to the great opinion
That Rome holds of his name; wherein obscurely
Caesar's ambition shall be glanced at.
And after this, let Caesar seat him sure,
For we will shake him, or worse days endure.

[*Exit*.]

SCENE-III — The same. A street

Thunder and lightning. Enter, from opposite sides, CASCA *with his sword drawn, and* CICERO.

CICERO Good even, Casca: brought you Caesar home?
Why are you breathless, and why stare you so?

CASCA Are not you moved, when all the sway of earth
Shakes like a thing unfirm? O Cicero,
I have seen tempests, when the scolding winds
Have riv'd the knotty oaks; and I have seen
Th' ambitious ocean swell and rage and foam,
To be exalted with the threatening clouds:
But never till tonight, never till now,
Did I go through a tempest dropping fire.
Either there is a civil strife in heaven,
Or else the world too saucy with the gods,
Incenses them to send destruction.

CICERO Why, saw you anything more wonderful?

CASCA A common slave, you'd know him well by sight,
Held up his left hand, which did flame and burn
Like twenty torches join'd, and yet his hand,
Not sensible of fire remain'd unscorch'd.
Besides, I ha' not since put up my sword,
Against the Capitol I met a lion,
Who glared upon me, and went surly by,
Without annoying me. And there were drawn
Upon a heap a hundred ghastly women,
Transformed with their fear; who swore they saw
Men, all in fire, walk up and down the streets.
And yesterday the bird of night did sit,
Even at noonday upon the marketplace,

Hooting and shrieking. When these prodigies
Do so conjointly meet, let not men say,
"These are their reasons; they are natural";
For I believe, they are portentous things
Unto the climate that they point upon.

CICERO Indeed, it is a strange-disposed time.
But men may construe things after their fashion,
Clean from the purpose of the things themselves.
Comes Caesar to the Capitol tomorrow?

CASCA He doth, for he did bid Antonius
Send word to you he would be there tomorrow.

CICERO Goodnight then, Casca: this disturbed sky
Is not to walk in.

CASCA Farewell, Cicero.

[*Exit* CICERO.]

Enter CASSIUS.

CASSIUS Who's there?

CASCA A Roman.

CASSIUS Casca, by your voice.

CASCA Your ear is good. Cassius, what night is this!

CASSIUS A very pleasing night to honest men.

CASCA Who ever knew the heavens menace so?

CASSIUS Those that have known the earth so full of faults.
For my part, I have walk'd about the streets,
Submitting me unto the perilous night;
And, thus unbraced, Casca, as you see,
Have bar'd my bosom to the thunder-stone;
And when the cross blue lightning seem'd to open
The breast of heaven, I did present myself
Even in the aim and very flash of it.

CASCA But wherefore did you so much tempt the Heavens?
It is the part of men to fear and tremble,
When the most mighty gods by tokens send
Such dreadful heralds to astonish us.

CASSIUS You are dull, Casca; and those sparks of life
That should be in a Roman you do want,

Or else you use not. You look pale and gaze,
And put on fear and cast yourself in wonder,
To see the strange impatience of the Heavens:
But if you would consider the true cause
Why all these fires, why all these gliding ghosts,
Why birds and beasts, from quality and kind;
Why old men, fools, and children calculate,
Why all these things change from their ordinance,
Their natures, and pre-formed faculties,
To monstrous quality; why, you shall find
That Heaven hath infus'd them with these spirits,
To make them instruments of fear and warning
Unto some monstrous state.
Now could I, Casca, name to thee a man
Most like this dreadful night,
That thunders, lightens, opens graves, and roars,
As doth the lion in the Capitol;
A man no mightier than thyself, or me,
In personal action; yet prodigious grown,
And fearful, as these strange eruptions are.

CASCA 'Tis Caesar that you mean; is it not, Cassius?

CASSIUS Let it be who it is: for Romans now
Have thews and limbs like to their ancestors;
But, woe the while! our fathers' minds are dead,
And we are govern'd with our mothers' spirits;
Our yoke and sufferance show us womanish.

CASCA Indeed, they say the senators tomorrow
Mean to establish Caesar as a king;
And he shall wear his crown by sea and land,
In every place, save here in Italy.

CASSIUS I know where I will wear this dagger then;
Cassius from bondage will deliver Cassius:
Therein, ye gods, you make the weak most strong;
Therein, ye gods, you tyrants do defeat.
Nor stony tower, nor walls of beaten brass,
Nor airless dungeon, nor strong links of iron,
Can be retentive to the strength of spirit;
But life, being weary of these worldly bars,
Never lacks power to dismiss itself.

If I know this, know all the world besides,
That part of tyranny that I do bear
I can shake off at pleasure.

[*Thunder still.*]

CASCA So can I:
So every bondman in his own hand bears
The power to cancel his captivity.

CASSIUS And why should Caesar be a tyrant then?
Poor man! I know he would not be a wolf,
But that he sees the Romans are but sheep:
He were no lion, were not Romans hinds.
Those that with haste will make a mighty fire
Begin it with weak straws. What trash is Rome,
What rubbish, and what offal, when it serves
For the base matter to illuminate
So vile a thing as Caesar! But, O grief,
Where hast thou led me? I, perhaps, speak this
Before a willing bondman: then I know
My answer must be made; but I am arm'd,
And dangers are to me indifferent.

CASCA You speak to Casca, and to such a man
That is no fleering tell-tale. Hold, my hand:
Be factious for redress of all these griefs,
And I will set this foot of mine as far
As who goes farthest.

CASSIUS There's a bargain made.
Now know you, Casca, I have mov'd already
Some certain of the noblest-minded Romans
To undergo with me an enterprise
Of honourable-dangerous consequence;
And I do know by this, they stay for me
In Pompey's Porch: for now, this fearful night,
There is no stir or walking in the streets;
And the complexion of the element
In favour's like the work we have in hand,
Most bloody, fiery, and most terrible.

Enter CINNA.

CASCA Stand close awhile, for here comes one in haste.

CASSIUS 'Tis Cinna; I do know him by his gait;
He is a friend. Cinna, where haste you so?

CINNA To find out you. Who's that? Metellus Cimber?

CASSIUS No, it is Casca, one incorporate
To our attempts. Am I not stay'd for, Cinna?

CINNA I am glad on't. What a fearful night is this!
There's two or three of us have seen strange sights.

CASSIUS Am I not stay'd for? tell me.

CINNA Yes, you are. O Cassius, if you could
But win the noble Brutus to our party—

CASSIUS Be you content. Good Cinna, take this paper,
And look you lay it in the praetor's chair,
Where Brutus may but find it; and throw this
In at his window; set this up with wax
Upon old Brutus' statue: all this done,
Repair to Pompey's Porch, where you shall find us.
Is Decius Brutus and Trebonius there?

CINNA All but Metellus Cimber, and he's gone
To seek you at your house. Well, I will hie,
And so bestow these papers as you bade me.

CASSIUS That done, repair to Pompey's theatre.

[*Exit* CINNA.]

Come, Casca, you and I will yet, ere day,
See Brutus at his house: three parts of him
Is ours already, and the man entire
Upon the next encounter, yields him ours.

CASCA O, he sits high in all the people's hearts!
And that which would appear offence in us,
His countenance, like richest alchemy,
Will change to virtue and to worthiness.

CASSIUS Him, and his worth, and our great need of him,
You have right well conceited. Let us go,
For it is after midnight; and ere day,
We will awake him, and be sure of him.

[*Exeunt.*]

ACT-II
SCENE-I — Rome. Brutus' orchard

Enter BRUTUS.

BRUTUS What, Lucius, ho!
I cannot, by the progress of the stars,
Give guess how near to day.—Lucius, I say!
I would it were my fault to sleep so soundly.
When, Lucius, when? Awake, I say! What, Lucius!

Enter LUCIUS.

LUCIUS Call'd you, my lord?

BRUTUS Get me a taper in my study, Lucius:
When it is lighted, come and call me here.

LUCIUS I will, my lord.

[*Exit.*]

BRUTUS It must be by his death: and for my part,
I know no personal cause to spurn at him,
But for the general. He would be crown'd:
How that might change his nature, there's the question.
It is the bright day that brings forth the adder,
And that craves wary walking. Crown him?—that;
And then, I grant, we put a sting in him,
That at his will he may do danger with.
Th' abuse of greatness is, when it disjoins
Remorse from power; and, to speak truth of Caesar,
I have not known when his affections sway'd
More than his reason. But 'tis a common proof,
That lowliness is young ambition's ladder,
Whereto the climber-upward turns his face;

But when he once attains the upmost round,
He then unto the ladder turns his back,
Looks in the clouds, scorning the base degrees
By which he did ascend. So Caesar may;
Then lest he may, prevent. And since the quarrel
Will bear no colour for the thing he is,
Fashion it thus: that what he is, augmented,
Would run to these and these extremities:
And therefore think him as a serpent's egg
Which hatch'd, would, as his kind grow mischievous;
And kill him in the shell.

Enter LUCIUS.

LUCIUS The taper burneth in your closet, sir.
Searching the window for a flint, I found
This paper, thus seal'd up, and I am sure
It did not lie there when I went to bed.

[*Gives him the letter.*]

BRUTUS Get you to bed again; it is not day.
Is not tomorrow, boy, the Ides of March?

LUCIUS I know not, sir.

BRUTUS Look in the calendar, and bring me word.

LUCIUS I will, sir.

[*Exit.*]

BRUTUS The exhalations, whizzing in the air
Give so much light that I may read by them.

[*Opens the letter and reads.*]

Brutus, thou sleep'st: awake and see thyself.
Shall Rome, &c. Speak, strike, redress!

"Brutus, thou sleep'st: awake!"
Such instigations have been often dropp'd
Where I have took them up.
"Shall Rome, &c." Thus must I piece it out:
Shall Rome stand under one man's awe? What, Rome?
My ancestors did from the streets of Rome
The Tarquin drive, when he was call'd a king.
"Speak, strike, redress!" Am I entreated

To speak and strike? O Rome, I make thee promise,
If the redress will follow, thou receivest
Thy full petition at the hand of Brutus.

Enter LUCIUS.

LUCIUS Sir, March is wasted fifteen days.

[*Knock within.*]

BRUTUS 'Tis good. Go to the gate, somebody knocks.

[*Exit Lucius.*]

Since Cassius first did whet me against Caesar,
I have not slept.
Between the acting of a dreadful thing
And the first motion, all the interim is
Like a phantasma, or a hideous dream:
The genius and the mortal instruments
Are then in council; and the state of man,
Like to a little kingdom, suffers then
The nature of an insurrection.

Enter LUCIUS.

LUCIUS Sir, 'tis your brother Cassius at the door,
Who doth desire to see you.

BRUTUS Is he alone?

LUCIUS No, sir, there are moe with him.

BRUTUS Do you know them?

LUCIUS No, sir, their hats are pluck'd about their ears,
And half their faces buried in their cloaks,
That by no means I may discover them
By any mark of favour.

BRUTUS Let 'em enter.

[*Exit* LUCIUS.]

They are the faction. O conspiracy,
Sham'st thou to show thy dangerous brow by night,
When evils are most free? O, then, by day
Where wilt thou find a cavern dark enough
To mask thy monstrous visage? Seek none, conspiracy;
Hide it in smiles and affability:

For if thou path, thy native semblance on,
Not Erebus itself were dim enough
To hide thee from prevention.

Enter CASSIUS, CASCA, DECIUS, CINNA, METELLUS CIMBER *and* TREBONIUS.

CASSIUS I think we are too bold upon your rest:
Good morrow, Brutus; do we trouble you?

BRUTUS I have been up this hour, awake all night.
Know I these men that come along with you?

CASSIUS Yes, every man of them; and no man here
But honours you; and everyone doth wish
You had but that opinion of yourself
Which every noble Roman bears of you.
This is Trebonius.

BRUTUS He is welcome hither.

CASSIUS This Decius Brutus.

BRUTUS He is welcome too.

CASSIUS This, Casca; this, Cinna; and this, Metellus Cimber.

BRUTUS They are all welcome.
What watchful cares do interpose themselves
Betwixt your eyes and night?

CASSIUS Shall I entreat a word?

[*They whisper.*]

DECIUS Here lies the east: doth not the day break here?

CASCA No.

CINNA O, pardon, sir, it doth; and yon grey lines
That fret the clouds are messengers of day.

CASCA You shall confess that you are both deceiv'd.
Here, as I point my sword, the Sun arises;
Which is a great way growing on the South,
Weighing the youthful season of the year.
Some two months hence, up higher toward the North
He first presents his fire; and the high East
Stands, as the Capitol, directly here.

BRUTUS Give me your hands all over, one by one.

CASSIUS And let us swear our resolution.

BRUTUS No, not an oath. If not the face of men,
The sufferance of our souls, the time's abuse—
If these be motives weak, break off betimes,
And every man hence to his idle bed.
So let high-sighted tyranny range on,
Till each man drop by lottery. But if these,
As I am sure they do, bear fire enough
To kindle cowards, and to steel with valour
The melting spirits of women; then, countrymen,
What need we any spur but our own cause
To prick us to redress? what other bond
Than secret Romans, that have spoke the word,
And will not palter? and what other oath
Than honesty to honesty engag'd,
That this shall be, or we will fall for it?
Swear priests and cowards, and men cautelous,
Old feeble carrions, and such suffering souls
That welcome wrongs; unto bad causes swear
Such creatures as men doubt; but do not stain
The even virtue of our enterprise,
Nor th' insuppressive mettle of our spirits,
To think that or our cause or our performance
Did need an oath; when every drop of blood
That every Roman bears, and nobly bears,
Is guilty of a several bastardy,
If he do break the smallest particle
Of any promise that hath pass'd from him.

CASSIUS But what of Cicero? Shall we sound him?
I think he will stand very strong with us.

CASCA Let us not leave him out.

CINNA No, by no means.

METELLUS O, let us have him, for his silver hairs
Will purchase us a good opinion,
And buy men's voices to commend our deeds.
It shall be said, his judgment rul'd our hands;
Our youths and wildness shall no whit appear,
But all be buried in his gravity.

BRUTUS O, name him not; let us not break with him;
For he will never follow anything
That other men begin.

CASSIUS Then leave him out.

CASCA Indeed, he is not fit.

DECIUS Shall no man else be touch'd but only Caesar?

CASSIUS Decius, well urg'd. I think it is not meet,
Mark Antony, so well belov'd of Caesar,
Should outlive Caesar: we shall find of him
A shrewd contriver; and you know, his means,
If he improve them, may well stretch so far
As to annoy us all; which to prevent,
Let Antony and Caesar fall together.

BRUTUS Our course will seem too bloody, Caius Cassius,
To cut the head off, and then hack the limbs,
Like wrath in death, and envy afterwards;
For Antony is but a limb of Caesar.
Let us be sacrificers, but not butchers, Caius.
We all stand up against the spirit of Caesar,
And in the spirit of men there is no blood.
O, that we then could come by Caesar's spirit,
And not dismember Caesar! But, alas,
Caesar must bleed for it! And, gentle friends,
Let's kill him boldly, but not wrathfully;
Let's carve him as a dish fit for the gods,
Not hew him as a carcass fit for hounds.
And let our hearts, as subtle masters do,
Stir up their servants to an act of rage,
And after seem to chide 'em. This shall mark
Our purpose necessary, and not envious;
Which so appearing to the common eyes,
We shall be call'd purgers, not murderers.
And for Mark Antony, think not of him;
For he can do no more than Caesar's arm
When Caesar's head is off.

CASSIUS Yet I fear him;
For in the ingrafted love he bears to Caesar—

BRUTUS Alas, good Cassius, do not think of him:
If he love Caesar, all that he can do

Is to himself; take thought and die for Caesar.
And that were much he should; for he is given
To sports, to wildness, and much company.

TREBONIUS There is no fear in him; let him not die;
For he will live, and laugh at this hereafter.

[*Clock strikes.*]

BRUTUS Peace! count the clock.

CASSIUS The clock hath stricken three.

TREBONIUS 'Tis time to part.

CASSIUS But it is doubtful yet
Whether Caesar will come forth today or no;
For he is superstitious grown of late,
Quite from the main opinion he held once
Of fantasy, of dreams, and ceremonies.
It may be these apparent prodigies,
The unaccustom'd terror of this night,
And the persuasion of his augurers,
May hold him from the Capitol today.

DECIUS Never fear that: if he be so resolved,
I can o'ersway him, for he loves to hear
That unicorns may be betray'd with trees,
And bears with glasses, elephants with holes,
Lions with toils, and men with flatterers.
But when I tell him he hates flatterers,
He says he does, being then most flattered.
Let me work;
For I can give his humour the true bent,
And I will bring him to the Capitol.

CASSIUS Nay, we will all of us be there to fetch him.

BRUTUS By the eighth hour: is that the uttermost?

CINNA Be that the uttermost; and fail not then.

METELLUS Caius Ligarius doth bear Caesar hard,
Who rated him for speaking well of Pompey;
I wonder none of you have thought of him.

BRUTUS Now, good Metellus, go along by him:
He loves me well, and I have given him reason;
Send him but hither, and I'll fashion him.

CASSIUS The morning comes upon's. We'll leave you, Brutus.
And, friends, disperse yourselves; but all remember
What you have said, and show yourselves true Romans.

BRUTUS Good gentlemen, look fresh and merrily;
Let not our looks put on our purposes,
But bear it as our Roman actors do,
With untired spirits and formal constancy.
And so, good morrow to you everyone.

[*Exeunt all but* BRUTUS.]

Boy! Lucius! Fast asleep? It is no matter;
Enjoy the honey-heavy dew of slumber:
Thou hast no figures nor no fantasies,
Which busy care draws in the brains of men;
Therefore thou sleep'st so sound.

Enter PORTIA.

PORTIA Brutus, my lord.

BRUTUS Portia, what mean you? Wherefore rise you now?
It is not for your health thus to commit
Your weak condition to the raw cold morning.

PORTIA Nor for yours neither. Y' have ungently, Brutus,
Stole from my bed; and yesternight at supper,
You suddenly arose, and walk'd about,
Musing and sighing, with your arms across;
And when I ask'd you what the matter was,
You star'd upon me with ungentle looks.
I urg'd you further; then you scratch'd your head,
And too impatiently stamp'd with your foot;
Yet I insisted, yet you answer'd not,
But with an angry wafture of your hand
Gave sign for me to leave you. So I did,
Fearing to strengthen that impatience
Which seem'd too much enkindled; and withal
Hoping it was but an effect of humour,
Which sometime hath his hour with every man.
It will not let you eat, nor talk, nor sleep;
And could it work so much upon your shape
As it hath much prevail'd on your condition,

I should not know you, Brutus. Dear my lord,
Make me acquainted with your cause of grief.

BRUTUS I am not well in health, and that is all.

PORTIA Brutus is wise, and, were he not in health,
He would embrace the means to come by it.

BRUTUS Why, so I do. Good Portia, go to bed.

PORTIA Is Brutus sick, and is it physical
To walk unbraced and suck up the humours
Of the dank morning? What, is Brutus sick,
And will he steal out of his wholesome bed
To dare the vile contagion of the night,
And tempt the rheumy and unpurged air
To add unto his sickness? No, my Brutus;
You have some sick offence within your mind,
Which, by the right and virtue of my place,
I ought to know of: and, upon my knees,
I charm you, by my once commended beauty,
By all your vows of love, and that great vow
Which did incorporate and make us one,
That you unfold to me, your self, your half,
Why you are heavy, and what men tonight
Have had resort to you; for here have been
Some six or seven, who did hide their faces
Even from darkness.

BRUTUS Kneel not, gentle Portia.

PORTIA I should not need, if you were gentle Brutus.
Within the bond of marriage, tell me, Brutus,
Is it excepted I should know no secrets
That appertain to you? Am I your self
But, as it were, in sort or limitation,
To keep with you at meals, comfort your bed,
And talk to you sometimes? Dwell I but in the suburbs
Of your good pleasure? If it be no more,
Portia is Brutus' harlot, not his wife.

BRUTUS You are my true and honourable wife,
As dear to me as are the ruddy drops
That visit my sad heart.

PORTIA If this were true, then should I know this secret.
I grant I am a woman; but withal
A woman that Lord Brutus took to wife;
I grant I am a woman; but withal
A woman well reputed, Cato's daughter.
Think you I am no stronger than my sex,
Being so father'd and so husbanded?
Tell me your counsels, I will not disclose 'em.
I have made strong proof of my constancy,
Giving myself a voluntary wound
Here, in the thigh: can I bear that with patience
And not my husband's secrets?

BRUTUS O ye gods,
Render me worthy of this noble wife!

[*Knock.*]

Hark, hark, one knocks. Portia, go in awhile;
And by and by thy bosom shall partake
The secrets of my heart.
All my engagements I will construe to thee,
All the charactery of my sad brows.
Leave me with haste.

[*Exit* PORTIA.]

Enter LUCIUS *with* LIGARIUS.

Lucius, who's that knocks?

LUCIUS Here is a sick man that would speak with you.

BRUTUS Caius Ligarius, that Metellus spake of.
Boy, stand aside. Caius Ligarius, how?

LIGARIUS Vouchsafe good-morrow from a feeble tongue.

BRUTUS O, what a time have you chose out, brave Caius,
To wear a kerchief! Would you were not sick!

LIGARIUS I am not sick, if Brutus have in hand
Any exploit worthy the name of honour.

BRUTUS Such an exploit have I in hand, Ligarius,
Had you a healthful ear to hear of it.

LIGARIUS By all the gods that Romans bow before,
I here discard my sickness. Soul of Rome!

Brave son, derived from honourable loins!
Thou, like an exorcist, hast conjur'd up
My mortified spirit. Now bid me run,
And I will strive with things impossible,
Yea, get the better of them. What's to do?

BRUTUS A piece of work that will make sick men whole.

LIGARIUS But are not some whole that we must make sick?

BRUTUS That must we also. What it is, my Caius,
I shall unfold to thee, as we are going,
To whom it must be done.

LIGARIUS Set on your foot,
And with a heart new-fir'd I follow you,
To do I know not what; but it sufficeth
That Brutus leads me on.

[*Thunder.*]

BRUTUS Follow me then.

[*Exeunt.*]

SCENE-II — A room in Caesar's palace

Thunder and lightning. Enter CAESAR, *in his nightgown.*

CAESAR — Nor heaven nor earth have been at peace tonight:
Thrice hath Calphurnia in her sleep cried out,
"Help, ho! They murder Caesar!" Who's within?

Enter a SERVANT.

SERVANT — My lord?

CAESAR — Go bid the priests do present sacrifice,
And bring me their opinions of success.

SERVANT — I will, my lord.

[*Exit.*]

Enter CALPHURNIA.

CALPHURNIA — What mean you, Caesar? Think you to walk forth?
You shall not stir out of your house today.

CAESAR — Caesar shall forth. The things that threaten'd me
Ne'er look'd but on my back; when they shall see
The face of Caesar, they are vanished.

CALPHURNIA — Caesar, I never stood on ceremonies,
Yet now they fright me. There is one within,
Besides the things that we have heard and seen,
Recounts most horrid sights seen by the watch.
A lioness hath whelped in the streets,
And graves have yawn'd, and yielded up their dead;
Fierce fiery warriors fight upon the clouds
In ranks and squadrons and right form of war,
Which drizzled blood upon the Capitol;
The noise of battle hurtled in the air,
Horses did neigh, and dying men did groan,

	And ghosts did shriek and squeal about the streets. O Caesar, these things are beyond all use, And I do fear them!
CAESAR	What can be avoided Whose end is purpos'd by the mighty gods? Yet Caesar shall go forth; for these predictions Are to the world in general as to Caesar.
CALPHURNIA	When beggars die, there are no comets seen; The heavens themselves blaze forth the death of princes.
CAESAR	Cowards die many times before their deaths; The valiant never taste of death but once. Of all the wonders that I yet have heard, It seems to me most strange that men should fear, Seeing that death, a necessary end, Will come when it will come.

Enter SERVANT.

	What say the augurers?
SERVANT	They would not have you to stir forth today. Plucking the entrails of an offering forth, They could not find a heart within the beast.
CAESAR	The gods do this in shame of cowardice: Caesar should be a beast without a heart If he should stay at home today for fear. No, Caesar shall not. Danger knows full well That Caesar is more dangerous than he. We are two lions litter'd in one day, And I the elder and more terrible, And Caesar shall go forth.
CALPHURNIA	Alas, my lord, Your wisdom is consum'd in confidence. Do not go forth today: call it my fear That keeps you in the house, and not your own. We'll send Mark Antony to the Senate-house, And he shall say you are not well today. Let me upon my knee prevail in this.
CAESAR	Mark Antony shall say I am not well, And for thy humour, I will stay at home.

Enter DECIUS.

Here's Decius Brutus, he shall tell them so.

DECIUS Caesar, all hail! Good morrow, worthy Caesar.
I come to fetch you to the Senate-house.

CAESAR And you are come in very happy time
To bear my greeting to the Senators,
And tell them that I will not come today.
Cannot, is false; and that I dare not, falser:
I will not come today. Tell them so, Decius.

CALPHURNIA Say he is sick.

CAESAR Shall Caesar send a lie?
Have I in conquest stretch'd mine arm so far,
To be afeard to tell grey-beards the truth?
Decius, go tell them Caesar will not come.

DECIUS Most mighty Caesar, let me know some cause,
Lest I be laugh'd at when I tell them so.

CAESAR The cause is in my will; I will not come.
That is enough to satisfy the Senate.
But for your private satisfaction,
Because I love you, I will let you know:
Calphurnia here, my wife, stays me at home.
She dreamt tonight she saw my statue,
Which like a fountain with an hundred spouts
Did run pure blood; and many lusty Romans
Came smiling, and did bathe their hands in it.
And these does she apply for warnings and portents
And evils imminent; and on her knee
Hath begg'd that I will stay at home today.

DECIUS This dream is all amiss interpreted:
It was a vision fair and fortunate.
Your statue spouting blood in many pipes,
In which so many smiling Romans bath'd,
Signifies that from you great Rome shall suck
Reviving blood, and that great men shall press
For tinctures, stains, relics, and cognizance.
This by Calphurnia's dream is signified.

CAESAR And this way have you well expounded it.

DECIUS I have, when you have heard what I can say;
And know it now. The Senate have concluded
To give this day a crown to mighty Caesar.
If you shall send them word you will not come,
Their minds may change. Besides, it were a mock
Apt to be render'd, for someone to say,
"Break up the Senate till another time,
When Caesar's wife shall meet with better dreams."
If Caesar hide himself, shall they not whisper
"Lo, Caesar is afraid"?
Pardon me, Caesar; for my dear dear love
To your proceeding bids me tell you this,
And reason to my love is liable.

CAESAR How foolish do your fears seem now, Calphurnia!
I am ashamed I did yield to them.
Give me my robe, for I will go.

Enter BRUTUS, LIGARIUS, METELLUS, CASCA, TREBONIUS, CINNA *and* PUBLIUS.

And look where Publius is come to fetch me.

PUBLIUS Good morrow, Caesar.

CAESAR Welcome, Publius.
What, Brutus, are you stirr'd so early too?
Good morrow, Casca. Caius Ligarius,
Caesar was ne'er so much your enemy
As that same ague which hath made you lean.
What is't o'clock?

BRUTUS Caesar, 'tis strucken eight.

CAESAR I thank you for your pains and courtesy.

Enter ANTONY.

See! Antony, that revels long a-nights,
Is notwithstanding up. Good morrow, Antony.

ANTONY So to most noble Caesar.

CAESAR Bid them prepare within.
I am to blame to be thus waited for.
Now, Cinna; now, Metellus; what, Trebonius!

I have an hour's talk in store for you:
Remember that you call on me today;
Be near me, that I may remember you.

TREBONIUS Caesar, I will. [*Aside.*] and so near will I be,
That your best friends shall wish I had been further.

CAESAR Good friends, go in, and taste some wine with me;
And we, like friends, will straightway go together.

BRUTUS [*Aside.*] That every like is not the same, O Caesar,
The heart of Brutus yearns to think upon.

[*Exeunt.*]

SCENE-III — A street near the Capitol

Enter ARTEMIDORUS, *reading a paper.*

ARTEMIDORUS *"Caesar, beware of Brutus; take heed of Cassius; come not near Casca; have an eye to Cinna; trust not Trebonius; mark well Metellus Cimber; Decius Brutus loves thee not; thou hast wrong'd Caius Ligarius. There is but one mind in all these men, and it is bent against Caesar. If thou be'st not immortal, look about you: security gives way to conspiracy. The mighty gods defend thee!*

Thy lover, Artemidorus."
Here will I stand till Caesar pass along,
And as a suitor will I give him this.
My heart laments that virtue cannot live
Out of the teeth of emulation.
If thou read this, O Caesar, thou mayest live;
If not, the Fates with traitors do contrive.

[*Exit.*]

SCENE-IV — Another part of the same street, before the house of Brutus

Enter PORTIA *and* LUCIUS.

PORTIA
I pr'ythee, boy, run to the Senate-house;
Stay not to answer me, but get thee gone.
Why dost thou stay?

LUCIUS
To know my errand, madam.

PORTIA
I would have had thee there and here again,
Ere I can tell thee what thou shouldst do there.
[*Aside.*] O constancy, be strong upon my side,
Set a huge mountain 'tween my heart and tongue!
I have a man's mind, but a woman's might.
How hard it is for women to keep counsel!
Art thou here yet?

LUCIUS
Madam, what should I do?
Run to the Capitol, and nothing else?
And so return to you, and nothing else?

PORTIA
Yes, bring me word, boy, if thy lord look well,
For he went sickly forth: and take good note
What Caesar doth, what suitors press to him.
Hark, boy, what noise is that?

LUCIUS
I hear none, madam.

PORTIA
Pr'ythee, listen well.
I heard a bustling rumour, like a fray,
And the wind brings it from the Capitol.

LUCIUS
Sooth, madam, I hear nothing.

Enter the SOOTHSAYER.

PORTIA Come hither, fellow:
Which way hast thou been?

SOOTHSAYER At mine own house, good lady.

PORTIA What is't o'clock?

SOOTHSAYER About the ninth hour, lady.

PORTIA Is Caesar yet gone to the Capitol?

SOOTHSAYER Madam, not yet. I go to take my stand,
To see him pass on to the Capitol.

PORTIA Thou hast some suit to Caesar, hast thou not?

SOOTHSAYER That I have, lady, if it will please Caesar
To be so good to Caesar as to hear me,
I shall beseech him to befriend himself.

PORTIA Why, know'st thou any harm's intended towards him?

SOOTHSAYER None that I know will be, much that I fear may chance.
Good morrow to you. Here the street is narrow.
The throng that follows Caesar at the heels,
Of Senators, of Praetors, common suitors,
Will crowd a feeble man almost to death:
I'll get me to a place more void, and there
Speak to great Caesar as he comes along.

[*Exit.*]

PORTIA I must go in.
[*Aside.*] Ay me, how weak a thing
The heart of woman is! O Brutus,
The heavens speed thee in thine enterprise!
Sure, the boy heard me. Brutus hath a suit
That Caesar will not grant. O, I grow faint.
Run, Lucius, and commend me to my lord;
Say I am merry; come to me again,
And bring me word what he doth say to thee.

[*Exeunt.*]

ACT-III

SCENE-I — Rome. Before the Capitol; the Senate sitting

A crowd of people in the street leading to the Capitol. FLOURISH. *Enter* CAESAR, BRUTUS, CASSIUS, CASCA, DECIUS, METELLUS, TREBONIUS, CINNA, ANTONY, LEPIDUS, ARTEMIDORUS, PUBLIUS, POPILIUS *and the* SOOTHSAYER.

CAESAR The Ides of March are come.

SOOTHSAYER Ay, Caesar; but not gone.

ARTEMIDORUS Hail, Caesar! Read this schedule.

DECIUS Trebonius doth desire you to o'er-read,
At your best leisure, this his humble suit.

ARTEMIDORUS O Caesar, read mine first; for mine's a suit
That touches Caesar nearer. Read it, great Caesar.

CAESAR What touches us ourself shall be last serv'd.

ARTEMIDORUS Delay not, Caesar. Read it instantly.

CAESAR What, is the fellow mad?

PUBLIUS Sirrah, give place.

CASSIUS What, urge you your petitions in the street?
Come to the Capitol.

CAESAR *enters the Capitol, the rest following. All the Senators rise.*

POPILIUS I wish your enterprise today may thrive.

CASSIUS What enterprise, Popilius?

POPILIUS Fare you well.

[*Advances to* CAESAR.]

BRUTUS What said Popilius Lena?

CASSIUS He wish'd today our enterprise might thrive.
I fear our purpose is discovered.

BRUTUS Look how he makes to Caesar: mark him.

CASSIUS Casca, be sudden, for we fear prevention.
Brutus, what shall be done? If this be known,
Cassius or Caesar never shall turn back,
For I will slay myself.

BRUTUS Cassius, be constant:
Popilius Lena speaks not of our purposes;
For look, he smiles, and Caesar doth not change.

CASSIUS Trebonius knows his time, for look you, Brutus,
He draws Mark Antony out of the way.

[*Exeunt* ANTONY *and* TREBONIUS. CAESAR *and the Senators take their seats.*]

DECIUS Where is Metellus Cimber? Let him go,
And presently prefer his suit to Caesar.

BRUTUS He is address'd; press near and second him.

CINNA Casca, you are the first that rears your hand.

CAESAR Are we all ready? What is now amiss
That Caesar and his Senate must redress?

METELLUS Most high, most mighty, and most puissant Caesar,
Metellus Cimber throws before thy seat
An humble heart.

[*Kneeling.*]

CAESAR I must prevent thee, Cimber.
These couchings and these lowly courtesies
Might fire the blood of ordinary men,
And turn pre-ordinance and first decree
Into the law of children. Be not fond,
To think that Caesar bears such rebel blood
That will be thaw'd from the true quality
With that which melteth fools; I mean sweet words,
Low-crooked curtsies, and base spaniel fawning.
Thy brother by decree is banished:
If thou dost bend, and pray, and fawn for him,

I spurn thee like a cur out of my way.
Know, Caesar dost not wrong, nor without cause
Will he be satisfied.

METELLUS Is there no voice more worthy than my own,
To sound more sweetly in great Caesar's ear
For the repealing of my banish'd brother?

BRUTUS I kiss thy hand, but not in flattery, Caesar;
Desiring thee that Publius Cimber may
Have an immediate freedom of repeal.

CAESAR What, Brutus?

CASSIUS Pardon, Caesar; Caesar, pardon:
As low as to thy foot doth Cassius fall,
To beg enfranchisement for Publius Cimber.

CAESAR I could be well mov'd, if I were as you;
If I could pray to move, prayers would move me:
But I am constant as the northern star,
Of whose true-fix'd and resting quality
There is no fellow in the firmament.
The skies are painted with unnumber'd sparks,
They are all fire, and every one doth shine;
But there's but one in all doth hold his place.
So in the world; 'tis furnish'd well with men,
And men are flesh and blood, and apprehensive;
Yet in the number I do know but one
That unassailable holds on his rank,
Unshak'd of motion: and that I am he,
Let me a little show it, even in this,
That I was constant Cimber should be banish'd,
And constant do remain to keep him so.

CINNA O Caesar,—

CAESAR Hence! wilt thou lift up Olympus?

DECIUS Great Caesar,—

CAESAR Doth not Brutus bootless kneel?

CASCA Speak, hands, for me!

[CASCA *stabs* CAESAR *in the neck.* CAESAR *catches hold of his arm. He is then stabbed by several other Conspirators, and at last by* MARCUS BRUTUS.]

CAESAR *Et tu, Brute?*—Then fall, Caesar!

[*Dies. The Senators and People retire in confusion.*]

CINNA Liberty! Freedom! Tyranny is dead!
Run hence, proclaim, cry it about the streets.

CASSIUS Some to the common pulpits and cry out,
"Liberty, freedom, and enfranchisement!"

BRUTUS People and Senators, be not affrighted.
Fly not; stand still; ambition's debt is paid.

CASCA Go to the pulpit, Brutus.

DECIUS And Cassius too.

BRUTUS Where's Publius?

CINNA Here, quite confounded with this mutiny.

METELLUS Stand fast together, lest some friend of Caesar's
Should chance—

BRUTUS Talk not of standing. Publius, good cheer!
There is no harm intended to your person,
Nor to no Roman else. So tell them, Publius.

CASSIUS And leave us, Publius; lest that the people
Rushing on us, should do your age some mischief.

BRUTUS Do so; and let no man abide this deed
But we the doers.

Enter TREBONIUS.

CASSIUS Where's Antony?

TREBONIUS Fled to his house amaz'd.
Men, wives, and children stare, cry out, and run,
As it were doomsday.

BRUTUS Fates, we will know your pleasures.
That we shall die, we know; 'tis but the time
And drawing days out, that men stand upon.

CASCA Why, he that cuts off twenty years of life
Cuts off so many years of fearing death.

BRUTUS Grant that, and then is death a benefit:
So are we Caesar's friends, that have abridg'd
His time of fearing death. Stoop, Romans, stoop,
And let us bathe our hands in Caesar's blood
Up to the elbows, and besmear our swords:

Then walk we forth, even to the market-place,
And waving our red weapons o'er our heads,
Let's all cry, "Peace, freedom, and liberty!"

CASSIUS

Stoop then, and wash. How many ages hence
Shall this our lofty scene be acted over
In States unborn, and accents yet unknown!

BRUTUS

How many times shall Caesar bleed in sport,
That now on Pompey's basis lies along,
No worthier than the dust!

CASSIUS

So oft as that shall be,
So often shall the knot of us be call'd
The men that gave their country liberty.

DECIUS

What, shall we forth?

CASSIUS

Ay, every man away.
Brutus shall lead; and we will grace his heels
With the most boldest and best hearts of Rome.

Enter a SERVANT.

BRUTUS

Soft, who comes here? A friend of Antony's.

SERVANT

Thus, Brutus, did my master bid me kneel;
Thus did Mark Antony bid me fall down;
And, being prostrate, thus he bade me say:
Brutus is noble, wise, valiant, and honest;
Caesar was mighty, bold, royal, and loving;
Say I love Brutus and I honour him;
Say I fear'd Caesar, honour'd him, and lov'd him.
If Brutus will vouchsafe that Antony
May safely come to him, and be resolv'd
How Caesar hath deserv'd to lie in death,
Mark Antony shall not love Caesar dead
So well as Brutus living; but will follow
The fortunes and affairs of noble Brutus
Thorough the hazards of this untrod state,
With all true faith. So says my master Antony.

BRUTUS

Thy master is a wise and valiant Roman;
I never thought him worse.
Tell him, so please him come unto this place,
He shall be satisfied and, by my honour,
Depart untouch'd.

SERVANT I'll fetch him presently.

[*Exit.*]

BRUTUS I know that we shall have him well to friend.

CASSIUS I wish we may: but yet have I a mind
That fears him much; and my misgiving still
Falls shrewdly to the purpose.

Enter ANTONY.

BRUTUS But here comes Antony. Welcome, Mark Antony.

ANTONY O mighty Caesar! Dost thou lie so low?
Are all thy conquests, glories, triumphs, spoils,
Shrunk to this little measure? Fare thee well.
I know not, gentlemen, what you intend,
Who else must be let blood, who else is rank:
If I myself, there is no hour so fit
As Caesar's death's hour; nor no instrument
Of half that worth as those your swords, made rich
With the most noble blood of all this world.
I do beseech ye, if you bear me hard,
Now, whilst your purpled hands do reek and smoke,
Fulfill your pleasure. Live a thousand years,
I shall not find myself so apt to die.
No place will please me so, no means of death,
As here by Caesar, and by you cut off,
The choice and master spirits of this age.

BRUTUS O Antony, beg not your death of us.
Though now we must appear bloody and cruel,
As by our hands and this our present act
You see we do; yet see you but our hands
And this the bleeding business they have done.
Our hearts you see not; they are pitiful;
And pity to the general wrong of Rome—
As fire drives out fire, so pity pity—
Hath done this deed on Caesar. For your part,
To you our swords have leaden points, Mark Antony;
Our arms in strength of malice, and our hearts
Of brothers' temper, do receive you in
With all kind love, good thoughts, and reverence.

CASSIUS Your voice shall be as strong as any man's
In the disposing of new dignities.

BRUTUS Only be patient till we have appeas'd
The multitude, beside themselves with fear,
And then we will deliver you the cause
Why I, that did love Caesar when I struck him,
Have thus proceeded.

ANTONY I doubt not of your wisdom.
Let each man render me his bloody hand.
First, Marcus Brutus, will I shake with you;
Next, Caius Cassius, do I take your hand.
Now, Decius Brutus, yours; now yours, Metellus;
Yours, Cinna; and, my valiant Casca, yours;
Though last, not least in love, yours, good Trebonius.
Gentlemen all—alas, what shall I say?
My credit now stands on such slippery ground,
That one of two bad ways you must conceit me,
Either a coward or a flatterer.
That I did love thee, Caesar, O, 'tis true:
If then thy spirit look upon us now,
Shall it not grieve thee dearer than thy death,
To see thy Antony making his peace,
Shaking the bloody fingers of thy foes,
Most noble, in the presence of thy corse?
Had I as many eyes as thou hast wounds,
Weeping as fast as they stream forth thy blood,
It would become me better than to close
In terms of friendship with thine enemies.
Pardon me, Julius! Here wast thou bay'd, brave hart;
Here didst thou fall; and here thy hunters stand,
Sign'd in thy spoil, and crimson'd in thy lethe.
O world, thou wast the forest to this hart;
And this indeed, O world, the heart of thee.
How like a deer strucken by many princes,
Dost thou here lie!

CASSIUS Mark Antony,—

ANTONY Pardon me, Caius Cassius:
The enemies of Caesar shall say this;
Then, in a friend, it is cold modesty.

CASSIUS I blame you not for praising Caesar so;
But what compact mean you to have with us?
Will you be prick'd in number of our friends,
Or shall we on, and not depend on you?

ANTONY Therefore I took your hands; but was indeed
Sway'd from the point, by looking down on Caesar.
Friends am I with you all, and love you all,
Upon this hope, that you shall give me reasons
Why, and wherein, Caesar was dangerous.

BRUTUS Or else were this a savage spectacle.
Our reasons are so full of good regard
That were you, Antony, the son of Caesar,
You should be satisfied.

ANTONY That's all I seek,
And am moreover suitor that I may
Produce his body to the market-place;
And in the pulpit, as becomes a friend,
Speak in the order of his funeral.

BRUTUS You shall, Mark Antony.

CASSIUS Brutus, a word with you.
[*Aside to Brutus.*] You know not what you do. Do not consent
That Antony speak in his funeral.
Know you how much the people may be mov'd
By that which he will utter?

BRUTUS [*Aside to Cassius.*] By your pardon:
I will myself into the pulpit first,
And show the reason of our Caesar's death.
What Antony shall speak, I will protest
He speaks by leave and by permission;
And that we are contented Caesar shall
Have all true rights and lawful ceremonies.
It shall advantage more than do us wrong.

CASSIUS [*Aside to Brutus.*] I know not what may fall; I like it not.

BRUTUS — Mark Antony, here, take you Caesar's body.
You shall not in your funeral speech blame us,
But speak all good you can devise of Caesar,
And say you do't by our permission;
Else shall you not have any hand at all
About his funeral. And you shall speak
In the same pulpit whereto I am going,
After my speech is ended.

ANTONY — Be it so;
I do desire no more.

BRUTUS — Prepare the body, then, and follow us.

[*Exeunt all but* ANTONY.]

ANTONY — O, pardon me, thou bleeding piece of earth,
That I am meek and gentle with these butchers.
Thou art the ruins of the noblest man
That ever lived in the tide of times.
Woe to the hand that shed this costly blood!
Over thy wounds now do I prophesy,
Which, like dumb mouths do ope their ruby lips
To beg the voice and utterance of my tongue,
A curse shall light upon the limbs of men;
Domestic fury and fierce civil strife
Shall cumber all the parts of Italy;
Blood and destruction shall be so in use,
And dreadful objects so familiar,
That mothers shall but smile when they behold
Their infants quartered with the hands of war;
All pity chok'd with custom of fell deeds:
And Caesar's spirit, ranging for revenge,
With Ate by his side come hot from Hell,
Shall in these confines with a monarch's voice
Cry havoc and let slip the dogs of war,
That this foul deed shall smell above the earth
With carrion men, groaning for burial.

Enter a SERVANT.

You serve Octavius Caesar, do you not?

SERVANT — I do, Mark Antony.

ANTONY — Caesar did write for him to come to Rome.

SERVANT He did receive his letters, and is coming,
And bid me say to you by word of mouth,—
[*Seeing the body.*] O Caesar!

ANTONY Thy heart is big, get thee apart and weep.
Passion, I see, is catching; for mine eyes,
Seeing those beads of sorrow stand in thine,
Began to water. Is thy master coming?

SERVANT He lies tonight within seven leagues of Rome.

ANTONY Post back with speed, and tell him what hath chanc'd.
Here is a mourning Rome, a dangerous Rome,
No Rome of safety for Octavius yet.
Hie hence, and tell him so. Yet stay awhile;
Thou shalt not back till I have borne this corse
Into the market-place: there shall I try,
In my oration, how the people take
The cruel issue of these bloody men;
According to the which thou shalt discourse
To young Octavius of the state of things.
Lend me your hand.

[*Exeunt with* CAESAR'S *body.*]

SCENE-II — The same. The Forum

Enter BRUTUS *and goes into the pulpit, and* CASSIUS, *with a throng of* CITIZENS.

CITIZENS — We will be satisfied; let us be satisfied.

BRUTUS — Then follow me, and give me audience, friends.
Cassius, go you into the other street
And part the numbers.
Those that will hear me speak, let 'em stay here;
Those that will follow Cassius, go with him;
And public reasons shall be rendered
Of Caesar's death.

FIRST CITIZEN — I will hear Brutus speak.

SECOND CITIZEN — I will hear Cassius; and compare their reasons,
When severally we hear them rendered.

[*Exit* CASSIUS, *with some of the Citizens.* BRUTUS *goes into the rostrum.*]

THIRD CITIZEN — The noble Brutus is ascended: silence!

BRUTUS — Be patient till the last.

Romans, countrymen, and lovers, hear me for my cause; and be silent, that you may hear. Believe me for mine honour, and have respect to mine honour, that you may believe. Censure me in your wisdom, and awake your senses, that you may the better judge. If there be any in this assembly, any dear friend of Caesar's, to him I say that Brutus' love to Caesar was no less than his. If then that friend demand why Brutus rose against Caesar, this is my answer: Not that I loved Caesar less, but that I loved Rome more.

Had you rather Caesar were living, and die all slaves, than that Caesar were dead, to live all free men? As Caesar loved me, I weep for him; as he was fortunate, I rejoice at it; as he was valiant, I honour him; but, as he was ambitious, I slew him. There is tears, for his love; joy for his fortune; honour for his valour; and death, for his ambition. Who is here so base, that would be a bondman? If any, speak; for him have I offended. Who is here so rude, that would not be a Roman? If any, speak; for him have I offended. Who is here so vile, that will not love his country? If any, speak; for him have I offended. I pause for a reply.

CITIZENS None, Brutus, none.

BRUTUS Then none have I offended. I have done no more to Caesar than you shall do to Brutus. The question of his death is enroll'd in the Capitol, his glory not extenuated, wherein he was worthy; nor his offences enforc'd, for which he suffered death.

Enter ANTONY *and others, with* CAESAR'S *body.*

Here comes his body, mourned by Mark Antony, who, though he had no hand in his death, shall receive the benefit of his dying, a place in the commonwealth; as which of you shall not? With this I depart, that, as I slew my best lover for the good of Rome, I have the same dagger for myself, when it shall please my country to need my death.

CITIZENS Live, Brutus! live, live!

FIRST CITIZEN Bring him with triumph home unto his house.

SECOND CITIZEN Give him a statue with his ancestors.

THIRD CITIZEN Let him be Caesar.

FOURTH CITIZEN Caesar's better parts
Shall be crown'd in Brutus.

FIRST CITIZEN We'll bring him to his house with shouts and clamours.

BRUTUS	My countrymen,—
SECOND CITIZEN	Peace! Silence! Brutus speaks.
FIRST CITIZEN	Peace, ho!
BRUTUS	Good countrymen, let me depart alone, And, for my sake, stay here with Antony. Do grace to Caesar's corpse, and grace his speech Tending to Caesar's glories, which Mark Antony, By our permission, is allow'd to make. I do entreat you, not a man depart, Save I alone, till Antony have spoke.
[*Exit.*]	
FIRST CITIZEN	Stay, ho! and let us hear Mark Antony.
THIRD CITIZEN	Let him go up into the public chair. We'll hear him. Noble Antony, go up.
ANTONY	For Brutus' sake, I am beholding to you.
[*Goes up.*]	
FOURTH CITIZEN	What does he say of Brutus?
THIRD CITIZEN	He says, for Brutus' sake He finds himself beholding to us all.
FOURTH CITIZEN	'Twere best he speak no harm of Brutus here!
FIRST CITIZEN	This Caesar was a tyrant.
THIRD CITIZEN	Nay, that's certain. We are blest that Rome is rid of him.
SECOND CITIZEN	Peace! let us hear what Antony can say.
ANTONY	You gentle Romans,—
CITIZENS	Peace, ho! let us hear him.
ANTONY	Friends, Romans, countrymen, lend me your ears; I come to bury Caesar, not to praise him. The evil that men do lives after them, The good is oft interred with their bones; So let it be with Caesar. The noble Brutus Hath told you Caesar was ambitious. If it were so, it was a grievous fault, And grievously hath Caesar answer'd it.

Here, under leave of Brutus and the rest,
For Brutus is an honourable man,
So are they all, all honourable men,
Come I to speak in Caesar's funeral.
He was my friend, faithful and just to me;
But Brutus says he was ambitious,
And Brutus is an honourable man.
He hath brought many captives home to Rome,
Whose ransoms did the general coffers fill:
Did this in Caesar seem ambitious?
When that the poor have cried, Caesar hath wept;
Ambition should be made of sterner stuff:
Yet Brutus says he was ambitious;
And Brutus is an honourable man.
You all did see that on the Lupercal
I thrice presented him a kingly crown,
Which he did thrice refuse. Was this ambition?
Yet Brutus says he was ambitious;
And sure he is an honourable man.
I speak not to disprove what Brutus spoke,
But here I am to speak what I do know.
You all did love him once, not without cause;
What cause withholds you then to mourn for him?
O judgment, thou art fled to brutish beasts,
And men have lost their reason. Bear with me.
My heart is in the coffin there with Caesar,
And I must pause till it come back to me.

FIRST CITIZEN Methinks there is much reason in his sayings.

SECOND CITIZEN If thou consider rightly of the matter,
Caesar has had great wrong.

THIRD CITIZEN Has he, masters?
I fear there will a worse come in his place.

FOURTH CITIZEN Mark'd ye his words? He would not take the crown;
Therefore 'tis certain he was not ambitious.

FIRST CITIZEN If it be found so, some will dear abide it.

SECOND CITIZEN Poor soul, his eyes are red as fire with weeping.

THIRD CITIZEN — There's not a nobler man in Rome than Antony.

FOURTH CITIZEN — Now mark him; he begins again to speak.

ANTONY — But yesterday the word of Caesar might
Have stood against the world; now lies he there,
And none so poor to do him reverence.
O masters! If I were dispos'd to stir
Your hearts and minds to mutiny and rage,
I should do Brutus wrong and Cassius wrong,
Who, you all know, are honourable men.
I will not do them wrong; I rather choose
To wrong the dead, to wrong myself and you,
Than I will wrong such honourable men.
But here's a parchment with the seal of Caesar,
I found it in his closet; 'tis his will:
Let but the commons hear this testament,
Which, pardon me, I do not mean to read,
And they would go and kiss dead Caesar's wounds,
And dip their napkins in his sacred blood;
Yea, beg a hair of him for memory,
And, dying, mention it within their wills,
Bequeathing it as a rich legacy
Unto their issue.

FOURTH CITIZEN — We'll hear the will. Read it, Mark Antony.

CITIZENS — The will, the will! We will hear Caesar's will.

ANTONY — Have patience, gentle friends, I must not read it.
It is not meet you know how Caesar loved you.
You are not wood, you are not stones, but men;
And being men, hearing the will of Caesar,
It will inflame you, it will make you mad.
'Tis good you know not that you are his heirs;
For if you should, O, what would come of it?

FOURTH CITIZEN — Read the will! We'll hear it, Antony;
You shall read us the will, Caesar's will!

ANTONY — Will you be patient? Will you stay awhile?
I have o'ershot myself to tell you of it.
I fear I wrong the honourable men
Whose daggers have stabb'd Caesar; I do fear it.

FOURTH CITIZEN They were traitors. Honourable men!

CITIZENS The will! The testament!

SECOND CITIZEN They were villains, murderers. The will! Read the will!

ANTONY You will compel me then to read the will?
Then make a ring about the corpse of Caesar,
And let me show you him that made the will.
Shall I descend? and will you give me leave?

CITIZENS Come down.

SECOND CITIZEN Descend.

[*He comes down.*]

THIRD CITIZEN You shall have leave.

FOURTH CITIZEN A ring! Stand round.

FIRST CITIZEN Stand from the hearse, stand from the body.

SECOND CITIZEN Room for Antony, most noble Antony!

ANTONY Nay, press not so upon me; stand far off.

CITIZENS Stand back; room! bear back.

ANTONY If you have tears, prepare to shed them now.
You all do know this mantle. I remember
The first time ever Caesar put it on;
'Twas on a Summer's evening, in his tent,
That day he overcame the Nervii.
Look, in this place ran Cassius' dagger through:
See what a rent the envious Casca made:
Through this the well-beloved Brutus stabb'd;
And as he pluck'd his cursed steel away,
Mark how the blood of Caesar follow'd it,
As rushing out of doors, to be resolv'd
If Brutus so unkindly knock'd, or no;
For Brutus, as you know, was Caesar's angel.
Judge, O you gods, how dearly Caesar lov'd him.
This was the most unkindest cut of all;
For when the noble Caesar saw him stab,
Ingratitude, more strong than traitors' arms,
Quite vanquish'd him: then burst his mighty heart;
And in his mantle muffling up his face,

Even at the base of Pompey's statue
Which all the while ran blood, great Caesar fell.
O, what a fall was there, my countrymen!
Then I, and you, and all of us fell down,
Whilst bloody treason flourish'd over us.
O, now you weep; and I perceive you feel
The dint of pity. These are gracious drops.
Kind souls, what weep you when you but behold
Our Caesar's vesture wounded? Look you here,
Here is himself, marr'd, as you see, with traitors.

FIRST CITIZEN O piteous spectacle!

SECOND CITIZEN O noble Caesar!

THIRD CITIZEN O woeful day!

FOURTH CITIZEN O traitors, villains!

FIRST CITIZEN O most bloody sight!

SECOND CITIZEN We will be revenged.

CITIZENS Revenge,—about,—seek,—burn,—fire,—kill,—slay,—let not a traitor live!

ANTONY Stay, countrymen.

FIRST CITIZEN Peace there! Hear the noble Antony.

SECOND CITIZEN We'll hear him, we'll follow him, we'll die with him.

ANTONY Good friends, sweet friends, let me not stir you up
To such a sudden flood of mutiny.
They that have done this deed are honourable.
What private griefs they have, alas, I know not,
That made them do it. They're wise and honourable,
And will, no doubt, with reasons answer you.
I come not, friends, to steal away your hearts.
I am no orator, as Brutus is;
But, as you know me all, a plain blunt man,
That love my friend; and that they know full well
That gave me public leave to speak of him.
For I have neither wit, nor words, nor worth,

Action, nor utterance, nor the power of speech,
To stir men's blood. I only speak right on.
I tell you that which you yourselves do know,
Show you sweet Caesar's wounds, poor poor dumb mouths,
And bid them speak for me. But were I Brutus,
And Brutus Antony, there were an Antony
Would ruffle up your spirits, and put a tongue
In every wound of Caesar, that should move
The stones of Rome to rise and mutiny.

CITIZENS We'll mutiny.

FIRST CITIZEN We'll burn the house of Brutus.

THIRD CITIZEN Away, then! come, seek the conspirators.

ANTONY Yet hear me, countrymen; yet hear me speak.

CITIZENS Peace, ho! Hear Antony; most noble Antony.

ANTONY Why, friends, you go to do you know not what.
Wherein hath Caesar thus deserved your loves?
Alas, you know not; I must tell you then.
You have forgot the will I told you of.

CITIZENS Most true; the will!—let's stay, and hear the will.

ANTONY Here is the will, and under Caesar's seal.
To every Roman citizen he gives,
To every several man, seventy-five drachmas.

SECOND CITIZEN Most noble Caesar! We'll revenge his death.

THIRD CITIZEN O, royal Caesar!

ANTONY Hear me with patience.

CITIZENS Peace, ho!

ANTONY Moreover, he hath left you all his walks,
His private arbors, and new-planted orchards,
On this side Tiber; he hath left them you,
And to your heirs forever; common pleasures,
To walk abroad, and recreate yourselves.
Here was a Caesar! when comes such another?

FIRST CITIZEN Never, never. Come, away, away!
We'll burn his body in the holy place,

And with the brands fire the traitors' houses.
Take up the body.

SECOND CITIZEN Go, fetch fire.

THIRD CITIZEN Pluck down benches.

FOURTH CITIZEN Pluck down forms, windows, anything.

[*Exeunt* CITIZENS, *with the body.*]

ANTONY Now let it work. Mischief, thou art afoot,
Take thou what course thou wilt!

Enter a SERVANT.

How now, fellow?

SERVANT Sir, Octavius is already come to Rome.

ANTONY Where is he?

SERVANT He and Lepidus are at Caesar's house.

ANTONY And thither will I straight to visit him.
He comes upon a wish. Fortune is merry,
And in this mood will give us anything.

SERVANT I heard him say Brutus and Cassius
Are rid like madmen through the gates of Rome.

ANTONY Belike they had some notice of the people,
How I had moved them. Bring me to Octavius.

[*Exeunt.*]

SCENE-III — The same. A street

Enter CINNA, *the poet, and after him the citizens.*

CINNA — I dreamt tonight that I did feast with Caesar,
And things unluckily charge my fantasy.
I have no will to wander forth of doors,
Yet something leads me forth.

FIRST CITIZEN — What is your name?

SECOND CITIZEN — Whither are you going?

THIRD CITIZEN — Where do you dwell?

FOURTH CITIZEN — Are you a married man or a bachelor?

SECOND CITIZEN — Answer every man directly.

FIRST CITIZEN — Ay, and briefly.

FOURTH CITIZEN — Ay, and wisely.

THIRD CITIZEN — Ay, and truly, you were best.

CINNA — What is my name? Whither am I going? Where do I dwell? Am I a married man or a bachelor? Then, to answer every man directly and briefly, wisely and truly. Wisely I say I am a bachelor.

SECOND CITIZEN — That's as much as to say they are fools that marry; you'll bear me a bang for that, I fear. Proceed, directly.

CINNA — Directly, I am going to Caesar's funeral.

FIRST CITIZEN — As a friend, or an enemy?

CINNA — As a friend.

SECOND CITIZEN — That matter is answered directly.

FOURTH CITIZEN — For your dwelling, briefly.

CINNA — Briefly, I dwell by the Capitol.

THIRD CITIZEN Your name, sir, truly.

CINNA Truly, my name is Cinna.

FIRST CITIZEN Tear him to pieces! He's a conspirator.

CINNA I am Cinna the poet, I am Cinna the poet.

FOURTH CITIZEN Tear him for his bad verses, tear him for his bad verses.

CINNA I am not Cinna the conspirator.

FOURTH CITIZEN It is no matter, his name's Cinna; pluck but his name out of his heart, and turn him going.

THIRD CITIZEN Tear him, tear him! Come; brands, ho! firebrands. To Brutus', to Cassius'; burn all. Some to Decius' house, and some to Casca's, some to Ligarius'. Away, go!

[*Exeunt.*]

ACT-IV
SCENE-I — Rome. A room in Antony's house

Enter ANTONY, OCTAVIUS *and* LEPIDUS, *seated at a table.*

ANTONY These many then shall die; their names are prick'd.

OCTAVIUS Your brother too must die; consent you, Lepidus?

LEPIDUS I do consent,—

OCTAVIUS Prick him down, Antony.

LEPIDUS Upon condition Publius shall not live,
Who is your sister's son, Mark Antony.

ANTONY He shall not live; look, with a spot I damn him.
But, Lepidus, go you to Caesar's house;
Fetch the will hither, and we shall determine
How to cut off some charge in legacies.

LEPIDUS What, shall I find you here?

OCTAVIUS Or here, or at the Capitol.

[*Exit* LEPIDUS.]

ANTONY This is a slight unmeritable man,
Meet to be sent on errands. Is it fit,
The three-fold world divided, he should stand
One of the three to share it?

OCTAVIUS So you thought him,
And took his voice who should be prick'd to die
In our black sentence and proscription.

ANTONY Octavius, I have seen more days than you;
And though we lay these honours on this man,
To ease ourselves of divers sland'rous loads,
He shall but bear them as the ass bears gold,

To groan and sweat under the business,
Either led or driven, as we point the way;
And having brought our treasure where we will,
Then take we down his load, and turn him off,
Like to the empty ass, to shake his ears,
And graze in commons.

OCTAVIUS You may do your will;
But he's a tried and valiant soldier.

ANTONY So is my horse, Octavius; and for that
I do appoint him store of provender.
It is a creature that I teach to fight,
To wind, to stop, to run directly on,
His corporal motion govern'd by my spirit.
And, in some taste, is Lepidus but so:
He must be taught, and train'd, and bid go forth:
A barren-spirited fellow; one that feeds
On objects, arts, and imitations,
Which, out of use and stal'd by other men,
Begin his fashion. Do not talk of him
But as a property. And now, Octavius,
Listen great things. Brutus and Cassius
Are levying powers; we must straight make head.
Therefore let our alliance be combin'd,
Our best friends made, our means stretch'd;
And let us presently go sit in council,
How covert matters may be best disclos'd,
And open perils surest answered.

OCTAVIUS Let us do so: for we are at the stake,
And bay'd about with many enemies;
And some that smile have in their hearts, I fear,
Millions of mischiefs.

[*Exeunt.*]

SCENE-II — Before Brutus' tent, in the camp near Sardis

Drum. Enter BRUTUS, LUCILIUS, TITINIUS *and* SOLDIERS; PINDARUS *meeting them;* LUCIUS *at some distance.*

BRUTUS
Stand, ho!

LUCILIUS
Give the word, ho! and stand.

BRUTUS
What now, Lucilius! is Cassius near?

LUCILIUS
He is at hand, and Pindarus is come
To do you salutation from his master.

[*Pindarus gives a letter to* BRUTUS.]

BRUTUS
He greets me well. Your master, Pindarus,
In his own change, or by ill officers,
Hath given me some worthy cause to wish
Things done, undone: but, if he be at hand,
I shall be satisfied.

PINDARUS
I do not doubt
But that my noble master will appear
Such as he is, full of regard and honour.

BRUTUS
He is not doubted. A word, Lucilius;
How he received you, let me be resolv'd.

LUCILIUS
With courtesy and with respect enough,
But not with such familiar instances,
Nor with such free and friendly conference,
As he hath us'd of old.

BRUTUS
Thou hast describ'd
A hot friend cooling. Ever note, Lucilius,
When love begins to sicken and decay
It useth an enforced ceremony.
There are no tricks in plain and simple faith;

But hollow men, like horses hot at hand,
Make gallant show and promise of their mettle;

[*Low march within.*]

But when they should endure the bloody spur,
They fall their crests, and like deceitful jades
Sink in the trial. Comes his army on?

LUCILIUS They meant this night in Sardis to be quarter'd;
The greater part, the horse in general,
Are come with Cassius.

Enter CASSIUS *and* SOLDIERS.

BRUTUS Hark! he is arriv'd.
March gently on to meet him.

CASSIUS Stand, ho!

BRUTUS Stand, ho! Speak the word along.

FIRST SOLDIER Stand!

SECOND SOLDIER Stand!

THIRD SOLDIER Stand!

CASSIUS Most noble brother, you have done me wrong.

BRUTUS Judge me, you gods; wrong I mine enemies?
And if not so, how should I wrong a brother?

CASSIUS Brutus, this sober form of yours hides wrongs;
And when you do them—

BRUTUS Cassius, be content.
Speak your griefs softly, I do know you well.
Before the eyes of both our armies here,
Which should perceive nothing but love from us,
Let us not wrangle. Bid them move away;
Then in my tent, Cassius, enlarge your griefs,
And I will give you audience.

CASSIUS Pindarus,
Bid our commanders lead their charges off
A little from this ground.

BRUTUS Lucilius, do you the like; and let no man
Come to our tent till we have done our conference.
Lucius and Titinius, guard our door.

[*Exeunt.*]

SCENE-III — Within the tent of Brutus

Enter BRUTUS *and* CASSIUS.

CASSIUS That you have wrong'd me doth appear in this:
You have condemn'd and noted Lucius Pella
For taking bribes here of the Sardians;
Wherein my letters, praying on his side
Because I knew the man, were slighted off.

BRUTUS You wrong'd yourself to write in such a case.

CASSIUS In such a time as this it is not meet
That every nice offence should bear his comment.

BRUTUS Let me tell you, Cassius, you yourself
Are much condemn'd to have an itching palm,
To sell and mart your offices for gold
To undeservers.

CASSIUS I an itching palm!
You know that you are Brutus that speak this,
Or, by the gods, this speech were else your last.

BRUTUS The name of Cassius honours this corruption,
And chastisement doth therefore hide his head.

CASSIUS Chastisement!

BRUTUS Remember March, the Ides of March remember:
Did not great Julius bleed for justice' sake?
What villain touch'd his body, that did stab,
And not for justice? What! Shall one of us,
That struck the foremost man of all this world
But for supporting robbers, shall we now
Contaminate our fingers with base bribes,
And sell the mighty space of our large honours
For so much trash as may be grasped thus?

I had rather be a dog, and bay the moon,
Than such a Roman.

CASSIUS Brutus, bait not me,
I'll not endure it. You forget yourself,
To hedge me in. I am a soldier, I,
Older in practice, abler than yourself
To make conditions.

BRUTUS Go to; you are not, Cassius.

CASSIUS I am.

BRUTUS I say you are not.

CASSIUS Urge me no more, I shall forget myself;
Have mind upon your health, tempt me no farther.

BRUTUS Away, slight man!

CASSIUS Is't possible?

BRUTUS Hear me, for I will speak.
Must I give way and room to your rash choler?
Shall I be frighted when a madman stares?

CASSIUS O ye gods, ye gods! Must I endure all this?

BRUTUS All this? ay, more: fret till your proud heart break;
Go show your slaves how choleric you are,
And make your bondmen tremble. Must I budge?
Must I observe you? Must I stand and crouch
Under your testy humour? By the gods,
You shall digest the venom of your spleen,
Though it do split you; for, from this day forth,
I'll use you for my mirth, yea, for my laughter,
When you are waspish.

CASSIUS Is it come to this?

BRUTUS You say you are a better soldier:
Let it appear so; make your vaunting true,
And it shall please me well. For mine own part,
I shall be glad to learn of noble men.

CASSIUS You wrong me every way, you wrong me, Brutus.
I said, an elder soldier, not a better:
Did I say better?

BRUTUS If you did, I care not.

CASSIUS When Caesar liv'd, he durst not thus have mov'd me.

BRUTUS Peace, peace! you durst not so have tempted him.

CASSIUS I durst not?

BRUTUS No.

CASSIUS What? durst not tempt him?

BRUTUS For your life you durst not.

CASSIUS Do not presume too much upon my love.
I may do that I shall be sorry for.

BRUTUS You have done that you should be sorry for.
There is no terror, Cassius, in your threats,
For I am arm'd so strong in honesty,
That they pass by me as the idle wind,
Which I respect not. I did send to you
For certain sums of gold, which you denied me;
For I can raise no money by vile means:
By Heaven, I had rather coin my heart,
And drop my blood for drachmas, than to wring
From the hard hands of peasants their vile trash
By any indirection. I did send
To you for gold to pay my legions,
Which you denied me: was that done like Cassius?
Should I have answer'd Caius Cassius so?
When Marcus Brutus grows so covetous,
To lock such rascal counters from his friends,
Be ready, gods, with all your thunderbolts,
Dash him to pieces!

CASSIUS I denied you not.

BRUTUS You did.

CASSIUS I did not. He was but a fool
That brought my answer back. Brutus hath riv'd my heart.
A friend should bear his friend's infirmities;
But Brutus makes mine greater than they are.

BRUTUS I do not, till you practise them on me.

CASSIUS You love me not.

BRUTUS I do not like your faults.

CASSIUS A friendly eye could never see such faults.

BRUTUS A flatterer's would not, though they do appear
As huge as high Olympus.

CASSIUS Come, Antony, and young Octavius, come,
Revenge yourselves alone on Cassius,
For Cassius is a-weary of the world:
Hated by one he loves; brav'd by his brother;
Check'd like a bondman; all his faults observ'd,
Set in a note-book, learn'd and conn'd by rote,
To cast into my teeth. O, I could weep
My spirit from mine eyes! There is my dagger,
And here my naked breast; within, a heart
Dearer than Plutus' mine, richer than gold:
If that thou be'st a Roman, take it forth.
I, that denied thee gold, will give my heart:
Strike as thou didst at Caesar; for I know,
When thou didst hate him worst, thou lovedst him better
Than ever thou lovedst Cassius.

BRUTUS Sheathe your dagger.
Be angry when you will, it shall have scope;
Do what you will, dishonour shall be humour.
O Cassius, you are yoked with a lamb
That carries anger as the flint bears fire,
Who, much enforced, shows a hasty spark,
And straight is cold again.

CASSIUS Hath Cassius liv'd
To be but mirth and laughter to his Brutus,
When grief and blood ill-temper'd vexeth him?

BRUTUS When I spoke that, I was ill-temper'd too.

CASSIUS Do you confess so much? Give me your hand.

BRUTUS And my heart too.

CASSIUS O Brutus!

BRUTUS What's the matter?

CASSIUS Have not you love enough to bear with me,
When that rash humour which my mother gave me
Makes me forgetful?

BRUTUS Yes, Cassius; and from henceforth,
When you are over-earnest with your Brutus,
He'll think your mother chides, and leave you so.

Enter POET, *followed by* LUCILIUS, TITINIUS *and* LUCIUS.

POET — [*Within.*] Let me go in to see the generals,
There is some grudge between 'em; 'tis not meet
They be alone.

LUCILIUS — [*Within.*] You shall not come to them.

POET — [*Within.*] Nothing but death shall stay me.

CASSIUS — How now! What's the matter?

POET — For shame, you generals! What do you mean?
Love, and be friends, as two such men should be;
For I have seen more years, I'm sure, than ye.

CASSIUS — Ha, ha! How vilely doth this cynic rhyme!

BRUTUS — Get you hence, sirrah. Saucy fellow, hence!

CASSIUS — Bear with him, Brutus; 'tis his fashion.

BRUTUS — I'll know his humour when he knows his time.
What should the wars do with these jigging fools?
Companion, hence!

CASSIUS — Away, away, be gone!

[*Exit* POET.]

BRUTUS — Lucilius and Titinius, bid the commanders
Prepare to lodge their companies tonight.

CASSIUS — And come yourselves and bring Messala with you
Immediately to us.

[*Exeunt* LUCILIUS *and* TITINIUS.]

BRUTUS — Lucius, a bowl of wine.

[*Exit* LUCIUS.]

CASSIUS — I did not think you could have been so angry.

BRUTUS — O Cassius, I am sick of many griefs.

CASSIUS — Of your philosophy you make no use,
If you give place to accidental evils.

BRUTUS — No man bears sorrow better. Portia is dead.

CASSIUS — Ha? Portia?

BRUTUS — She is dead.

CASSIUS — How 'scap'd I killing, when I cross'd you so?
O insupportable and touching loss!
Upon what sickness?

BRUTUS — Impatient of my absence,
And grief that young Octavius with Mark Antony
Have made themselves so strong; for with her death
That tidings came. With this she fell distract,
And, her attendants absent, swallow'd fire.

CASSIUS — And died so?

BRUTUS — Even so.

CASSIUS — O ye immortal gods!

Enter LUCIUS, *with wine and a taper.*

BRUTUS — Speak no more of her. Give me a bowl of wine.
In this I bury all unkindness, Cassius.

[*Drinks.*]

CASSIUS — My heart is thirsty for that noble pledge.
Fill, Lucius, till the wine o'erswell the cup.
I cannot drink too much of Brutus' love.

[Drinks.]

[*Exit* LUCIUS.]

Enter TITINIUS *and* MESSALA.

BRUTUS — Come in, Titinius!
Welcome, good Messala.
Now sit we close about this taper here,
And call in question our necessities.

CASSIUS — Portia, art thou gone?

BRUTUS — No more, I pray you.
Messala, I have here received letters,
That young Octavius and Mark Antony
Come down upon us with a mighty power,
Bending their expedition toward Philippi.

MESSALA — Myself have letters of the selfsame tenor.

BRUTUS — With what addition?

MESSALA — That by proscription and bills of outlawry
Octavius, Antony, and Lepidus
Have put to death an hundred Senators.

BRUTUS — Therein our letters do not well agree.
Mine speak of seventy Senators that died
By their proscriptions, Cicero being one.

CASSIUS Cicero one!

MESSALA Cicero is dead,
And by that order of proscription.
Had you your letters from your wife, my lord?

BRUTUS No, Messala.

MESSALA Nor nothing in your letters writ of her?

BRUTUS Nothing, Messala.

MESSALA That, methinks, is strange.

BRUTUS Why ask you? Hear you aught of her in yours?

MESSALA No, my lord.

BRUTUS Now as you are a Roman, tell me true.

MESSALA Then like a Roman bear the truth I tell,
For certain she is dead, and by strange manner.

BRUTUS Why, farewell, Portia. We must die, Messala.
With meditating that she must die once,
I have the patience to endure it now.

MESSALA Even so great men great losses should endure.

CASSIUS I have as much of this in art as you,
But yet my nature could not bear it so.

BRUTUS Well, to our work alive. What do you think
Of marching to Philippi presently?

CASSIUS I do not think it good.

BRUTUS Your reason?

CASSIUS This it is:
'Tis better that the enemy seek us;
So shall he waste his means, weary his soldiers,
Doing himself offence, whilst we, lying still,
Are full of rest, defence, and nimbleness.

BRUTUS Good reasons must of force give place to better.
The people 'twixt Philippi and this ground
Do stand but in a forced affection;
For they have grudg'd us contribution.
The enemy, marching along by them,
By them shall make a fuller number up,
Come on refresh'd, new-added, and encourag'd;
From which advantage shall we cut him off

If at Philippi we do face him there,
These people at our back.

CASSIUS Hear me, good brother.

BRUTUS Under your pardon. You must note besides,
That we have tried the utmost of our friends,
Our legions are brim-full, our cause is ripe.
The enemy increaseth every day;
We, at the height, are ready to decline.
There is a tide in the affairs of men,
Which, taken at the flood, leads on to fortune;
Omitted, all the voyage of their life
Is bound in shallows and in miseries.
On such a full sea are we now afloat,
And we must take the current when it serves,
Or lose our ventures.

CASSIUS Then, with your will, go on:
We'll along ourselves, and meet them at Philippi.

BRUTUS The deep of night is crept upon our talk,
And nature must obey necessity,
Which we will niggard with a little rest.
There is no more to say?

CASSIUS No more. Good night:
Early tomorrow will we rise, and hence.

Enter LUCIUS.

BRUTUS Lucius! My gown.

[*Exit* LUCIUS.]

Farewell now, good Messala.
Good night, Titinius. Noble, noble Cassius,
Good night, and good repose.

CASSIUS O my dear brother!
This was an ill beginning of the night.
Never come such division 'tween our souls!
Let it not, Brutus.

Enter LUCIUS *with the gown.*

BRUTUS Everything is well.

CASSIUS Good night, my lord.

BRUTUS Good night, good brother.

TITINIUS
and MESSALA Good night, Lord Brutus.

BRUTUS. Farewell, everyone.

[*Exeunt* CASSIUS, TITINIUS *and* MESSALA.]

Give me the gown. Where is thy instrument?

LUCIUS Here in the tent.

BRUTUS What, thou speak'st drowsily?
Poor knave, I blame thee not, thou art o'er-watch'd.
Call Claudius and some other of my men;
I'll have them sleep on cushions in my tent.

LUCIUS Varro and Claudius!

Enter VARRO *and* CLAUDIUS.

VARRO Calls my lord?

BRUTUS I pray you, sirs, lie in my tent and sleep;
It may be I shall raise you by-and-by
On business to my brother Cassius.

VARRO So please you, we will stand and watch your pleasure.

BRUTUS I will not have it so; lie down, good sirs,
It may be I shall otherwise bethink me.
Look, Lucius, here's the book I sought for so;
I put it in the pocket of my gown.

[*Servants lie down.*]

LUCIUS I was sure your lordship did not give it me.

BRUTUS Bear with me, good boy, I am much forgetful.
Canst thou hold up thy heavy eyes awhile,
And touch thy instrument a strain or two?

LUCIUS Ay, my lord, an't please you.

BRUTUS It does, my boy.
I trouble thee too much, but thou art willing.

LUCIUS It is my duty, sir.

BRUTUS I should not urge thy duty past thy might;
I know young bloods look for a time of rest.

LUCIUS — I have slept, my lord, already.

BRUTUS — It was well done, and thou shalt sleep again;
I will not hold thee long. If I do live,
I will be good to thee.

[LUCIUS *plays and sings till he falls asleep.*]

This is a sleepy tune. O murd'rous slumber,
Layest thou thy leaden mace upon my boy,
That plays thee music? Gentle knave, good night;
I will not do thee so much wrong to wake thee.
If thou dost nod, thou break'st thy instrument;
I'll take it from thee; and, good boy, good night.
Let me see, let me see; is not the leaf turn'd down
Where I left reading? Here it is, I think.

Enter the GHOST *of* CAESAR.

How ill this taper burns! Ha! who comes here?
I think it is the weakness of mine eyes
That shapes this monstrous apparition.
It comes upon me. Art thou anything?
Art thou some god, some angel, or some devil,
That mak'st my blood cold and my hair to stare?
Speak to me what thou art.

GHOST — Thy evil spirit, Brutus.

BRUTUS — Why com'st thou?

GHOST — To tell thee thou shalt see me at Philippi.

BRUTUS — Well; then I shall see thee again?

GHOST — Ay, at Philippi.

BRUTUS — Why, I will see thee at Philippi then.

[GHOST *vanishes.*]

Now I have taken heart, thou vanishest.
Ill spirit, I would hold more talk with thee.
Boy! Lucius! Varro! Claudius! Sirs, awake! Claudius!

LUCIUS — The strings, my lord, are false.

BRUTUS — He thinks he still is at his instrument.
Lucius, awake!

LUCIUS — My lord?

BRUTUS — Didst thou dream, Lucius, that thou so criedst out?

LUCIUS My lord, I do not know that I did cry.

BRUTUS Yes, that thou didst. Didst thou see anything?

LUCIUS Nothing, my lord.

BRUTUS Sleep again, Lucius. Sirrah Claudius!
Fellow thou, awake!

VARRO My lord?

CLAUDIUS My lord?

BRUTUS Why did you so cry out, sirs, in your sleep?

VARRO. CLAUDIUS Did we, my lord?

BRUTUS Ay. Saw you anything?

VARRO No, my lord, I saw nothing.

CLAUDIUS Nor I, my lord.

BRUTUS Go and commend me to my brother Cassius;
Bid him set on his powers betimes before,
And we will follow.

VARRO. CLAUDIUS It shall be done, my lord.

[*Exeunt.*]

ACT-V
SCENE-I — The plains of Philippi

Enter Octavius, Antony *and their Army.*

OCTAVIUS — Now, Antony, our hopes are answered.
You said the enemy would not come down,
But keep the hills and upper regions.
It proves not so; their battles are at hand,
They mean to warn us at Philippi here,
Answering before we do demand of them.

ANTONY — Tut, I am in their bosoms, and I know
Wherefore they do it. They could be content
To visit other places, and come down
With fearful bravery, thinking by this face
To fasten in our thoughts that they have courage;
But 'tis not so.

Enter a Messenger.

MESSENGER — Prepare you, generals.
The enemy comes on in gallant show;
Their bloody sign of battle is hung out,
And something to be done immediately.

ANTONY — Octavius, lead your battle softly on
Upon the left hand of the even field.

OCTAVIUS — Upon the right hand I. Keep thou the left.

ANTONY — Why do you cross me in this exigent?

OCTAVIUS — I do not cross you; but I will do so.

[*March.*]

Drum. Enter Brutus, Cassius *and their Army;* Lucilius, Titinius, Messala *and others.*

BRUTUS They stand, and would have parley.

CASSIUS Stand fast, Titinius; we must out and talk.

OCTAVIUS Mark Antony, shall we give sign of battle?

ANTONY No, Caesar, we will answer on their charge.
Make forth; the generals would have some words.

OCTAVIUS Stir not until the signal.

BRUTUS Words before blows: is it so, countrymen?

OCTAVIUS Not that we love words better, as you do.

BRUTUS Good words are better than bad strokes, Octavius.

ANTONY In your bad strokes, Brutus, you give good words;
Witness the hole you made in Caesar's heart,
Crying, "Long live! Hail, Caesar!"

CASSIUS Antony,
The posture of your blows are yet unknown;
But for your words, they rob the Hybla bees,
And leave them honeyless.

ANTONY Not stingless too.

BRUTUS O yes, and soundless too,
For you have stol'n their buzzing, Antony,
And very wisely threat before you sting.

ANTONY Villains, you did not so when your vile daggers
Hack'd one another in the sides of Caesar:
You show'd your teeth like apes, and fawn'd like hounds,
And bow'd like bondmen, kissing Caesar's feet;
Whilst damned Casca, like a cur, behind
Struck Caesar on the neck. O you flatterers!

CASSIUS Flatterers! Now, Brutus, thank yourself.
This tongue had not offended so today,
If Cassius might have rul'd.

OCTAVIUS Come, come, the cause. If arguing makes us sweat,
The proof of it will turn to redder drops.
Look, I draw a sword against conspirators.
When think you that the sword goes up again?
Never, till Caesar's three and thirty wounds
Be well aveng'd; or till another Caesar
Have added slaughter to the sword of traitors.

BRUTUS Caesar, thou canst not die by traitors' hands,
Unless thou bring'st them with thee.

OCTAVIUS So I hope.
I was not born to die on Brutus' sword.

BRUTUS O, if thou wert the noblest of thy strain,
Young man, thou couldst not die more honourable.

CASSIUS A peevish school-boy, worthless of such honour,
Join'd with a masker and a reveller.

ANTONY Old Cassius still!

OCTAVIUS Come, Antony; away!
Defiance, traitors, hurl we in your teeth.
If you dare fight today, come to the field;
If not, when you have stomachs.

[*Exeunt* OCTAVIUS, ANTONY *and their Army.*]

CASSIUS Why now, blow wind, swell billow, and swim bark!
The storm is up, and all is on the hazard.

BRUTUS Ho, Lucilius! Hark, a word with you.

LUCILIUS My lord?

[BRUTUS *and* LUCILIUS *talk apart.*]

CASSIUS Messala.

MESSALA What says my General?

CASSIUS Messala,
This is my birth-day; as this very day
Was Cassius born. Give me thy hand, Messala:
Be thou my witness that against my will
As Pompey was, am I compell'd to set
Upon one battle all our liberties.
You know that I held Epicurus strong,
And his opinion. Now I change my mind,
And partly credit things that do presage.
Coming from Sardis, on our former ensign
Two mighty eagles fell, and there they perch'd,
Gorging and feeding from our soldiers' hands,
Who to Philippi here consorted us.
This morning are they fled away and gone,
And in their steads do ravens, crows, and kites
Fly o'er our heads, and downward look on us,

As we were sickly prey: their shadows seem
A canopy most fatal, under which
Our army lies, ready to give up the ghost.

MESSALA Believe not so.

CASSIUS I but believe it partly,
For I am fresh of spirit, and resolv'd
To meet all perils very constantly.

BRUTUS Even so, Lucilius.

CASSIUS Now, most noble Brutus,
The gods today stand friendly, that we may,
Lovers in peace, lead on our days to age!
But, since the affairs of men rest still incertain,
Let's reason with the worst that may befall.
If we do lose this battle, then is this
The very last time we shall speak together:
What are you then determined to do?

BRUTUS Even by the rule of that philosophy
By which I did blame Cato for the death
Which he did give himself, I know not how,
But I do find it cowardly and vile,
For fear of what might fall, so to prevent
The time of life, arming myself with patience
To stay the providence of some high powers
That govern us below.

CASSIUS Then, if we lose this battle,
You are contented to be led in triumph
Thorough the streets of Rome?

BRUTUS No, Cassius, no: think not, thou noble Roman,
That ever Brutus will go bound to Rome;
He bears too great a mind. But this same day
Must end that work the Ides of March begun;
And whether we shall meet again I know not.
Therefore our everlasting farewell take.
For ever, and for ever, farewell, Cassius.
If we do meet again, why, we shall smile;
If not, why then this parting was well made.

CASSIUS For ever and for ever farewell, Brutus.
If we do meet again, we'll smile indeed;
If not, 'tis true this parting was well made.

BRUTUS Why then, lead on. O, that a man might know
The end of this day's business ere it come!
But it sufficeth that the day will end,
And then the end is known. Come, ho! away!

[*Exeunt.*]

SCENE-II — The same. The field of battle

Alarum. Enter BRUTUS *and* MESSALA.

BRUTUS Ride, ride, Messala, ride, and give these bills
Unto the legions on the other side.

[*Loud alarum.*]

Let them set on at once; for I perceive
But cold demeanor in Octavius' wing,
And sudden push gives them the overthrow.
Ride, ride, Messala; let them all come down.

[*Exeunt.*]

SCENE-III — Another part of the field

Alarum. Enter CASSIUS *and* TITINIUS.

CASSIUS
O, look, Titinius, look, the villains fly!
Myself have to mine own turn'd enemy:
This ensign here of mine was turning back;
I slew the coward, and did take it from him.

TITINIUS
O Cassius, Brutus gave the word too early,
Who, having some advantage on Octavius,
Took it too eagerly: his soldiers fell to spoil,
Whilst we by Antony are all enclos'd.

Enter PINDARUS.

PINDARUS
Fly further off, my lord, fly further off;
Mark Antony is in your tents, my lord.
Fly, therefore, noble Cassius, fly far off.

CASSIUS
This hill is far enough. Look, look, Titinius;
Are those my tents where I perceive the fire?

TITINIUS
They are, my lord.

CASSIUS
Titinius, if thou lovest me,
Mount thou my horse and hide thy spurs in him,
Till he have brought thee up to yonder troops
And here again, that I may rest assur'd
Whether yond troops are friend or enemy.

TITINIUS
I will be here again, even with a thought.

[*Exit.*]

CASSIUS
Go, Pindarus, get higher on that hill,
My sight was ever thick. Regard Titinius,
And tell me what thou notest about the field.

[*Pindarus goes up.*]

This day I breathed first. Time is come round,
And where I did begin, there shall I end.
My life is run his compass. Sirrah, what news?

PINDARUS [*Above.*] O my lord!

CASSIUS What news?

PINDARUS [*Above.*] Titinius is enclosed round about
With horsemen, that make to him on the spur,
Yet he spurs on. Now they are almost on him.
Now, Titinius! Now some light. O, he lights too.
He's ta'en!

[*Shout.*]

And, hark! they shout for joy.

CASSIUS Come down; behold no more.
O, coward that I am, to live so long,
To see my best friend ta'en before my face!

[*Pindarus descends.*]

Come hither, sirrah.
In Parthia did I take thee prisoner;
And then I swore thee, saving of thy life,
That whatsoever I did bid thee do,
Thou shouldst attempt it. Come now, keep thine oath.
Now be a freeman; and with this good sword,
That ran through Caesar's bowels, search this bosom.
Stand not to answer. Here, take thou the hilts;
And when my face is cover'd, as 'tis now,
Guide thou the sword.—Caesar, thou art reveng'd,
Even with the sword that kill'd thee.

[*Dies.*]

PINDARUS So, I am free, yet would not so have been,
Durst I have done my will. O Cassius!
Far from this country Pindarus shall run,
Where never Roman shall take note of him.

[*Exit.*]

Enter TITINIUS *with* MESSALA.

MESSALA It is but change, Titinius; for Octavius
Is overthrown by noble Brutus' power,
As Cassius' legions are by Antony.

TITINIUS These tidings would well comfort Cassius.

MESSALA Where did you leave him?

TITINIUS All disconsolate,
With Pindarus his bondman, on this hill.

MESSALA Is not that he that lies upon the ground?

TITINIUS He lies not like the living. O my heart!

MESSALA Is not that he?

TITINIUS No, this was he, Messala,
But Cassius is no more. O setting sun,
As in thy red rays thou dost sink to night,
So in his red blood Cassius' day is set.
The sun of Rome is set. Our day is gone;
Clouds, dews, and dangers come; our deeds are done.
Mistrust of my success hath done this deed.

MESSALA Mistrust of good success hath done this deed.
O hateful Error, Melancholy's child!
Why dost thou show to the apt thoughts of men
The things that are not? O Error, soon conceiv'd,
Thou never com'st unto a happy birth,
But kill'st the mother that engender'd thee!

TITINIUS What, Pindarus! where art thou, Pindarus?

MESSALA Seek him, Titinius, whilst I go to meet
The noble Brutus, thrusting this report
Into his ears. I may say thrusting it;
For piercing steel and darts envenomed
Shall be as welcome to the ears of Brutus
As tidings of this sight.

TITINIUS Hie you, Messala,
And I will seek for Pindarus the while.

[*Exit* MESSALA.]

Why didst thou send me forth, brave Cassius?
Did I not meet thy friends? And did not they
Put on my brows this wreath of victory,

And bid me give it thee? Didst thou not hear their shouts?
Alas, thou hast misconstrued everything!
But, hold thee, take this garland on thy brow;
Thy Brutus bid me give it thee, and I
Will do his bidding. Brutus, come apace,
And see how I regarded Caius Cassius.
By your leave, gods. This is a Roman's part.
Come, Cassius' sword, and find Titinius' heart.

[*Dies.*]

Alarum. Enter BRUTUS, MESSALA, YOUNG CATO, STRATO, VOLUMNIUS *and* LUCILIUS.

BRUTUS Where, where, Messala, doth his body lie?

MESSALA Lo, yonder, and Titinius mourning it.

BRUTUS Titinius' face is upward.

CATO He is slain.

BRUTUS O Julius Caesar, thou art mighty yet!
Thy spirit walks abroad, and turns our swords
In our own proper entrails.

[*Low alarums.*]

CATO Brave Titinius!
Look whether he have not crown'd dead Cassius!

BRUTUS Are yet two Romans living such as these?
The last of all the Romans, fare thee well!
It is impossible that ever Rome
Should breed thy fellow. Friends, I owe more tears
To this dead man than you shall see me pay.
I shall find time, Cassius, I shall find time.
Come therefore, and to Thassos send his body.
His funerals shall not be in our camp,
Lest it discomfort us. Lucilius, come;
And come, young Cato; let us to the field.
Labeo and Flavius, set our battles on.
'Tis three o'clock; and Romans, yet ere night
We shall try fortune in a second fight.

[*Exeunt.*]

SCENE-IV — Another part of the field

Alarum. Enter fighting soldiers of both armies; then BRUTUS, MESSALA, YOUNG CATO, LUCILIUS, FLAVIUS *and others.*

BRUTUS — Yet, countrymen, O, yet hold up your heads!

CATO — What bastard doth not? Who will go with me?
I will proclaim my name about the field.
I am the son of Marcus Cato, ho!
A foe to tyrants, and my country's friend.
I am the son of Marcus Cato, ho!

[*Charges the enemy.*]

LUCILIUS — And I am Brutus, Marcus Brutus, I;
Brutus, my country's friend; know me for Brutus!

[*Exit, charging the enemy.* CATO *is overpowered, and falls.*]

LUCILIUS — O young and noble Cato, art thou down?
Why, now thou diest as bravely as Titinius,
And mayst be honour'd, being Cato's son.

FIRST SOLDIER — Yield, or thou diest.

LUCILIUS — Only I yield to die:
There is so much that thou wilt kill me straight;

[*Offering money*]

Kill Brutus, and be honour'd in his death.

FIRST SOLDIER — We must not. A noble prisoner!

SECOND SOLDIER — Room, ho! Tell Antony, Brutus is ta'en.

FIRST SOLDIER — I'll tell the news. Here comes the General.

Enter ANTONY.

Brutus is ta'en, Brutus is ta'en, my lord.

ANTONY — Where is he?

LUCILIUS — Safe, Antony; Brutus is safe enough.
I dare assure thee that no enemy
Shall ever take alive the noble Brutus.
The gods defend him from so great a shame!
When you do find him, or alive or dead,
He will be found like Brutus, like himself.

ANTONY — This is not Brutus, friend; but, I assure you,
A prize no less in worth. Keep this man safe,
Give him all kindness. I had rather have
Such men my friends than enemies. Go on,
And see whether Brutus be alive or dead;
And bring us word unto Octavius' tent
How everything is chanc'd.

[*Exeunt.*]

SCENE-V — Another part of the field

Enter BRUTUS, DARDANIUS, CLITUS, STRATO *and* VOLUMNIUS.

BRUTUS Come, poor remains of friends, rest on this rock.

CLITUS Statilius show'd the torch-light; but, my lord,
He came not back: he is or ta'en or slain.

BRUTUS Sit thee down, Clitus. Slaying is the word;
It is a deed in fashion. Hark thee, Clitus.

[*Whispering.*]

CLITUS What, I, my lord? No, not for all the world.

BRUTUS Peace then, no words.

CLITUS I'll rather kill myself.

BRUTUS Hark thee, Dardanius.

[*Whispers him.*]

DARDANIUS Shall I do such a deed?

CLITUS O Dardanius!

DARDANIUS O Clitus!

CLITUS What ill request did Brutus make to thee?

DARDANIUS To kill him, Clitus. Look, he meditates.

CLITUS Now is that noble vessel full of grief,
That it runs over even at his eyes.

BRUTUS Come hither, good Volumnius; list a word.

VOLUMNIUS What says my lord?

BRUTUS Why, this, Volumnius:
The ghost of Caesar hath appear'd to me
Two several times by night; at Sardis once,
And this last night here in Philippi fields.
I know my hour is come.

VOLUMNIUS Not so, my lord.

BRUTUS Nay I am sure it is, Volumnius.
Thou seest the world, Volumnius, how it goes;
Our enemies have beat us to the pit.

[*Low alarums.*]

It is more worthy to leap in ourselves
Than tarry till they push us. Good Volumnius,
Thou know'st that we two went to school together;
Even for that our love of old, I pr'ythee
Hold thou my sword-hilts, whilst I run on it.

VOLUMNIUS That's not an office for a friend, my lord.

[*Alarums still.*]

CLITUS Fly, fly, my lord! there is no tarrying here.

BRUTUS Farewell to you; and you; and you, Volumnius.
Strato, thou hast been all this while asleep;
Farewell to thee too, Strato.—Countrymen,
My heart doth joy, that yet in all my life
I found no man but he was true to me.
I shall have glory by this losing day
More than Octavius and Mark Antony
By this vile conquest shall attain unto.
So fare you well at once; for Brutus' tongue
Hath almost ended his life's history.
Night hangs upon mine eyes; my bones would rest,
That have but labour'd to attain this hour.

[*Alarums. Cry within, "Fly, fly, fly!".*]

CLITUS Fly, my lord, fly!

BRUTUS Hence! I will follow.

[*Exeunt* CLITUS, DARDANIUS *and* VOLUMNIUS.]

I pr'ythee, Strato, stay thou by thy lord.
Thou art a fellow of a good respect;
Thy life hath had some smatch of honour in it.
Hold then my sword, and turn away thy face,
While I do run upon it. Wilt thou, Strato?

STRATO Give me your hand first. Fare you well, my lord.

BRUTUS Farewell, good Strato.—Caesar, now be still:
I kill'd not thee with half so good a will.

[He runs on his sword, and dies.]

Alarum. Retreat. Enter ANTONY, OCTAVIUS, MESSALA, LUCILIUS *and the Army.*

OCTAVIUS What man is that?

MESSALA My master's man. Strato, where is thy master?

STRATO Free from the bondage you are in, Messala.
The conquerors can but make a fire of him;
For Brutus only overcame himself,
And no man else hath honour by his death.

LUCILIUS So Brutus should be found. I thank thee, Brutus,
That thou hast prov'd Lucilius' saying true.

OCTAVIUS All that serv'd Brutus, I will entertain them.
Fellow, wilt thou bestow thy time with me?

STRATO Ay, if Messala will prefer me to you.

OCTAVIUS Do so, good Messala.

MESSALA How died my master, Strato?

STRATO I held the sword, and he did run on it.

MESSALA Octavius, then take him to follow thee,
That did the latest service to my master.

ANTONY This was the noblest Roman of them all.
All the conspirators save only he,
Did that they did in envy of great Caesar;
He only, in a general honest thought
And common good to all, made one of them.
His life was gentle, and the elements
So mix'd in him that Nature might stand up
And say to all the world, "This was a man!"

OCTAVIUS According to his virtue let us use him
With all respect and rites of burial.
Within my tent his bones tonight shall lie,
Most like a soldier, order'd honourably.
So call the field to rest, and let's away,
To part the glories of this happy day.

[Exeunt.]

* * *

www.ingramcontent.com/pod-product-compliance
Lightning Source LLC
LaVergne TN
LVHW101926220826
846093LV00009B/390

9789354629679